Air War over
SPAIN

Aviators, Aircraft and Air Units of the Nationalist and Republican Air Forces 1936-1939

BERMUY LÓPEZ (Translated from the Spanish by Juan Carlos Salgado)

Background to the Spanish Civil War

In order to understand the Spanish Civil War, it is necessary to describe the political background that led to its origin. By the early 1900s, Spain was divided into two mutually hostile social groups, with landowners and industrialists on one side and landless labourers on the other. The advance of Socialism and anarchism among urban workers led the more far-sighted landowners to try to stop the spread of this to the countryside. Counter-revolutionary syndicates were financed by landlords from 1906 and in 1912 a group of dynamic social Catholics led by Angel Herrera helped establish a series of powerful Agrarian Federations. These right-wing organisations tried to improve the lives of impoverished farmers by offering them credit facilities, agricultural expertise, warehousing and machinery in return for their adoption of virulent anti-socialism. Nevertheless left-wing urban unrest became so virulent that the army was forced to crush the striking Socialists in August 1917 in a bloody operation. The right-wing industrialists were still fearful of militant workers on the streets, however, and this forced them to drop their own political demands and join in a coalition government in 1918 with the Liberals and Conservatives.

The defeat of the urban Socialists in 1917 did not, however, mark the end of the attack on the right wing. Between 1918 and 1921 anarchist labourers from the south took part in a series of uprisings which, although crushed again by the army and civil guard, intensified social resentment in the rural south. The end of the First World War had resulted in a revival of foreign competition and a consequent recession in Spain. To counter this, the Catalonian industrialists in particular, introduced a series of wage cuts and lay offs. This resulted in a spiralling of urban violence, particularly in Barcelona.

On 23 September 1923 the right wing General, Miguel Primo de Rivera, Captain-General of Barcelona, carried out a *coup d'état* after having accused the parliamentary government of leading the country to ruin. King Alfonso XIII then entrusted the government to Primo de Rivera who, though arbitrary, was a dictator of some mildness and charm and outwardly restored order. A brief golden age began. The calm was superficial, however, and discontent increased. In January 1930, the King abruptly withdrew his support from Primo de Rivera. Alfonso then tried to return to the system of alternative moderate Liberal and Conservative governments, but these were unable to control the upsurge of left-wing Republicanism. In the municipal elections of April 1931 the Republicans won an overwhelming majority and Alfonso bowed to the result and left Spain.

Alcalá Zamora, an Andalusian, then became first prime minister of a moderate but weak provisional government which was incapable of maintaining order. Riots broke out all over Spain during which churches and convents were burned and looted. In June 1931 a constituent parliament was elected and the success of the Republican coalition was confirmed by the voters. Zamora was appointed president of Spain in December 1931, trying in vain to steer a middle course between the Left and Right.

For the following two years the country was governed by the Socialist Majority led by the Leftist writer and intellectual, Manuel Azaña. In August 1932 General José Sanjurjo led a right-wing military insurrection against this government, but it was crushed without difficulty. Elections were then held in November 1933 which resulted in the victory of the CEDA or Catholic Party led by José Maria Gil Robles. Relying on the support of various right-wing groups, the party was to trigger a revolution in October 1934 when Catalan Nationalists, Socialists and Asturian miners rose against it, giving a foretaste of what was to come. The revolution was brutally suppressed and Azaña imprisoned.

On 18 February 1936, hoping that a centre party would at last emerge between the warring political extremes, President Zamora called an election, but the Left Wing or Popular Front gained control of the country and Anzaña again became prime minister. The situation rapidly deteriorated. The state was powerless to deal with the violence of various antagonistic elements and had proved incapable of carrying out the necessary reforms. On 13 July 1936 a former Conservative minister and now effectively leader of the right-wing opposition, José Calvo Sotelo, was murdered two days after he was openly threatened by a Communist deputy. Four days later, a military uprising began, ostensibly with the aim of restoring order.

The first leader of the military backlash was General Emilio Mola and it was planned to make Sanjurjo – the leader of the earlier failed coup – the figurehead. Another of the conspirators was General Francisco Franco, who had earlier been relieved of his post as Chief of General Staff by the Republicans and made Governor of the Canary Islands. As the revolution developed, Franco was flown from the Canary Islands to Spanish Morocco which had already fallen to the Nationalists and where some 47,000 well-trained troops were based. On 19 July, Sanjurjo was killed when his aircraft crashed on take-off from Portugal, and this and other reasons led to Franco, who outranked Mola, becoming the preferred leader of the rebellion. By 22 July 1936, Spain was divided, with the Leftist Republicans in control of much of the south and east, plus a northern coastal strip including Oviedo, Santander and Bilbao, whilst the Nationalists held the remainder of the country plus the cities of Seville and Cadiz in the south.

CHAPTER ONE
The Spanish Second Republic and aviation

Reorganization

THE advent of the Spanish Second Republic in April 1931 brought about yet another change in Spanish aviation. For a long time, almost every shift in government in Madrid had involved some changes in aviation, either organic or legal, or in uniforms and other such areas.

Naturally, the new government placed the most pro-Republican airmen in leading posts within the aviation infrastructure: for example, those who had distinguished themselves in the December 1930 civil/military coup, when the rebel airmen at Cuatro Vientos air base in Madrid had been the key players.

After the failure of the coup, the main leaders fled to Portugal by air or were exiled to France, but they soon returned, although one of the results of the Cuatro Vientos attempt had been the disbandment of the promotion roster of the *Servicio de Aviación* – Aviation Service. It is true that the newly born Republic greatly sympathized with the *Aviación Militar* (Military Aviation), because of its pro-Republican stance. However, the government did not reinstate its own roster, did not make it an independent corps and simply provided it with a uniform of its own – this time a navy blue, a colour similar to that worn by personnel of the *Marina de Guerra* (Navy). *Aviación Militar* officers still functioned within the infantry, cavalry, artillery and engineer corps.

The Republic appointed aviation *comandante* Ramón Franco, of world-record fame and the brother of the future dictator, as *Director General de Aeronáutica*, although he was soon replaced by *capitán* Arturo Álvarez Buylla. Other airmen who had mutinied at Cuatro Vientos, such as Ángel Pastor or José Martínez de Aragón, were also popular with the Republican politicians and were raised to important positions.

As regards organization, the *Batallones de Aviación* (Aviation Battalions) established by the previous monarchist government, were disbanded and the four *Escuadras de Aviación* (Aviation Wings), which survived till the outbreak of the civil war, were established instead. The *4ª Escuadra* became the *Fuerzas Aéreas de África* – 'Africa Air Force'.

As far as air equipment was concerned, the licence-built Nieuport 52 C1 fighter series made by La Hispano Suiza in Guadalajara, the Breguet XIX reconnaissance and light bomber sesquiplanes made by Construcciones Aeronáuticas S.A. (C.A.S.A.), at Getafe, Madrid and the last Loring C.III

A factory-fresh Nieuport 52 photographed at the Hispano Suiza factory at Guadalajara.

AIR WAR OVER SPAIN

A Breguet XIX, s/n 211, of the last series built by Construcciones Aeronáuticas S.A. (C.A.S.A.), at Getafe, Madrid.

Two Nieuport 52s of Grupo de Caza nº 12. Note the jumping deer emblem on the fuselage beneath the cockpit. This unit had been disbanded a few days before the start of the Civil War.

reconnaissance aircraft, made by Loring at Carabanchel, Madrid were completed. Also the last Dornier *Wal* flying boats were completed at the Puntales workshops in Cadiz – premises belonging to C.A.S.A. – both for military use with the *Aviación Militar* and the *Aeronáutica Naval* (Naval Aviation) and for civil use.

These aircraft formed the standard equipment of the *Aviación Militar* units, along with the old training De Havilland DH-9s, Avro 504 Ks and Bristol F2Bs aircraft still in service with the flying schools.

The Spanish Republic also set about strengthening the other military branch of the *Aviación*, the *Aeronáutica Naval*, the naval air arm of the *Marina de Guerra*, and approved the definitive plan for the construction of the new *Base Aeronaval* at San Javier, Murcia and also the construction of 25 C.A.S.A. licence-built Vickers Vildebeest torpedo aircraft and Hispano E-30 trainers. Additionally, construction of the last Italian licence-built Savoia S-62 seaplane series continued at the *Aeronáutica Naval* Workshops in Barcelona.

Another great political task undertaken by the Republican government was the establishment of a state-owned air line, *Líneas Aéreas Postales Españolas* (L.A.P.E.), for passenger and mail transport, in order to link the Peninsula with the Balearic and Canary Islands. Several transport aircraft types were acquired for that purpose, such as the Dutch Fokker F.VII 3m and the American Ford F.5 trimotors and finally the novel Douglas DC-2 twin-engined aircraft.

Last but not least, a *Negociado de Propaganda Aérea* (Air Propaganda Bureau) was established in order to promote general public interest in aeronautics, to support the birth of sports aviation societies, aero clubs and private flying schools and to subsidise the acquisition of equipment for individuals and to obtain private pilot licences.

Forerunner to the Air Ministry

The year 1933 was very important both in military and aeronautical policies, as Manuel Azaña's government of *Izquierda Republicana* issued a decree on 5 April to create the *Dirección General de Aeronáutica* (General Department of Aeronautics), reorganizing the existing aeronautical services. This new organ was dependent on the cabinet's president and assumed the functions entrusted, until then, to the *Dirección General de Aeronáutica Civil* (General Department of Civil Aeronautics), the *Jefatura de Aviación Militar* (Military Aviation Command) of the War Ministry and the *Dirección de Aeronáutica Naval* (Naval Aviation Department) of the *Ministerio de Marina* (Navy Ministry). The *Servicio Meteorológico Nacional* (National Meteorological Service), which was previously subject to the *Instituto Geográfico y Catastral* (Geographical and Cadastral Institute), was also assigned to the *Dirección General*.

Under the jurisdiction of the cabinet's president, it was in charge of the superior command of the *Fuerzas Aéreas*, the training of civil and military *Aeronáutica* personnel, air traffic management, the

THE SPANISH SECOND REPUBLIC AND AVIATION

technical and industrial service of the *Aeronáutica* and the management of the corresponding budgets. Not integrated, however, were the *Aerostación Militar* (Military Aerostat) services, which remained subject to the *Ejército de Tierra* (Army).

The *Dirección General de Aeronáutica* was established with the following branches:

Secretaría (Secretariat)
Jefatura Superior de las Fuerzas del Aire (High Command of the Air Force)
Jefatura de Instrucción (Training Command)
Sección de Tráfico Aéreo (Air Traffic Branch)
Sección de Servicios Técnicos e Industriales (Technical and Industrial Service Branch)
Sección de Contabilidad y Presupuestos (Accountancy and Budget Branch)

A militarised L.A.P.E. Ford F.5 trimotor. Note the camouflage despite the EC-RRA civil registration. Behind the F.5 can be seen a 2ª Escuadrilla Polikarpov I-15.

Above left: An obsolete but seemingly tireless De Havilland DH-9 kept on flying at the Escuela de Observadores y ametralladores at Los Alcázares almost until the end of the Civil War.

The *Secretaría* was in charge of general affairs and those related to the internal regime of the *Dirección*, civil personnel and relationships with the Ministries and official or private branches for the purposes and services it was entrusted with. It also served as a liaison organ between the different branches of the *Dirección General* itself.

The *Jefatura de Instrucción* would also be in charge of managing the still-to-be formed *Escuela General de Aeronáutica* (General Department of Aeronautics) and an *Escuela Táctica Militar* (Military Tactical School), which was to establish training policy and oversee the operations of the civilian *Escuelas*.

The *Sección de Tráfico Aéreo*, which was responsible for all aspects of efficiency and safety, would embrace the *Servicio Meteorológico Nacional*, the *Servicio de Propaganda*, airports, domestic air lines, the *Servicio Aeropostal* (Airmail Service) and any matters related to foreign international air lines.

The *Sección de los Servicios Técnicos e Industriales* would be responsible for the *Escuela de Ingenieros Aeronáuticos* (Aeronautical Engineering School), scientific research, promotion of the national air industry, requests for prototypes, nationalization of patents and raw materials, acquisition of materiel and aeronautical construction of all kinds. The *Aeronáutica* technical personnel would also depend on this section.

The *Sección de Contabilidad y Presupuestos* was in charge of budgets for services entrusted to the *Dirección General* and administration of the corresponding funds.

For the first time ever in Spain, the term '*Fuerzas Aéreas*' – 'Air Force' – was used.[1] This was made up of the *Armada Aérea* (Air Fleet), the *Defensa Aérea* (Air Defence) and the respective cooperation aviations for the *Ejército de Tierra* and the *Marina*. The establishment of this *Armada Aérea* would be effected as soon as the *Cooperation* and *Defensa Aérea* aviations had the necessary elements to carry out their own functions.

The *Defensa Aérea* would be created simultaneously with that of the ground elements of the *Defensa Contra Aeronaves* (D.C.A. – Anti Aircraft Defence) belonging to the *Ejército*.

The *Cooperation* aviation for the *Ejército* would be made up of the air elements of the large ground organizations and those necessary for the ground defence of naval stations and the *Aviación de Cooperación Naval* would be based at the *Bases Aeronavales*, supplemented with units deployed on board warships.

Special regulations would determine the relevant missions of each of these organisations and each unit of the different aviation categories could, whenever service needs required, support and even be detached to another organization, if the *Consejo Superior de Aeronáutica* (Central Aeronautics Board) required it.

[1.] There was never an official acronym known as F.A.R.E. (*Fuerzas Aéreas de la República*); this is an invention of foreign writers during the 1980s.

AIR WAR OVER SPAIN

The Hawker Spanish Fury was the most modern fighter in the Aviación Militar. A locally-built series of 50 was planned. However, only three British-built Furies arrived in Spain before the war. (Warleta)

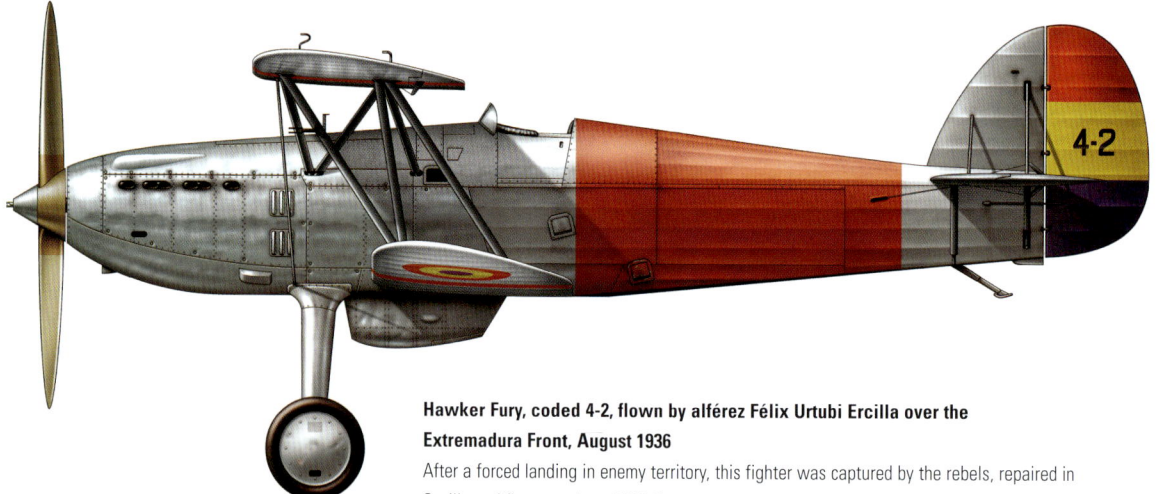

Hawker Fury, coded 4-2, flown by alférez Félix Urtubi Ercilla over the Extremadura Front, August 1936
After a forced landing in enemy territory, this fighter was captured by the rebels, repaired in Seville and flown again as '4W-1'.

The direct command of the *Fuerzas Aéreas* was assigned to a military chief who was appointed *Jefe Superior de las Fuerzas Aéreas*, and would exert direct command over the *Armada Aérea*, the *División de Defensa Aérea* (Air Defence Division) and its general services, as well as air, administration and technical inspection of the *Aviaciones de Cooperación* (Cooperation Aviation), whose deployment would be under the direct control of the military or naval commands they were assigned to. The chief of the *Fuerzas Aéreas* was to be assisted by a *Secretaría* and an *Estado Mayor* (Headquarters). He was to be in charge of the personnel, armament and ammunition, air and ground equipment, air bases, buildings and all other elements forming the *Fuerzas Aéreas*. The *Estado Mayor* was in charge of organization, intelligence, operations, mobilization and services of the *Fuerzas Aéreas*.

An *Escuela General de Aeronáutica* was established with the following purposes:

To supply the *Ejército de Tierra* and *Marina* with acceptable personnel, following theoretical and practical training after which they would be commissioned as aviation officers.

To train civil aviation pilots and officers.

An *Escuela Táctica General*, also built from scratch, would serve to provide training in different military specialities, and was to be made up of as many sections as necessary for the common or special tasks the personnel of the different aviation categories were to carry out.

Measures were later established which oversaw the senior and junior pilot officer personnel of the *Servicio de Aviación del Ejército* and which would issue guidelines for the creation of officer cadres of the different aviation categories and for the necessary requirements for those who wished to join the *Fuerzas Aéreas*.

THE SPANISH SECOND REPUBLIC AND AVIATION

The *Aviación Naval* officers were to remain as a *Servicio* and as part of the *Cuerpo General de la Armada*.

From then on, the *Fuerzas Aéreas* was to be expanded with personnel from the *Escuela General de Aeronáutica*, who had to pass the relevant courses at the *Escuela Táctica General*.

Those *Fuerzas Aéreas* personnel arriving from the *Ejército de Tierra* would serve in *Armada Aérea*, *Aviación de Defensa Aérea* and *Aviación de Cooperación con el Ejército* units, and those arriving from the *Servicio de la Aviación Naval*, in the *Aviación de Cooperación con la Marina* units. However, if temporary service needs required, all personnel could be deployed to any commitments that suited their trades.

The *Dirección General de Aeronáutica* recruited *Observadores Aéreos* (Air Observers) as well as aeronautical engineers, *Cuerpos Auxiliares* (Auxiliary Corps) personnel, specialists, subaltern personnel and *Aviación* troops and seamen.

This new legislation formed the basis for the establishment of a future Air Ministry, embracing not only military and naval, but also civil aviation, as in most other modern European countries.

Budgetary reasons and the coming of a new government, of a very different political persuasion, shattered Manuel Azaña's clear view by the year's end.

The modernisation of the Spanish *Aviación*

The arrival of *capitán* Ismael Warleta de la Quintana, a capable military technician – not a politician or a civil servant – at the *Dirección General de Aeronáutica* represented an attempt at modernization of the aircraft of the different types of aviation. In June 1935 it became evident that the Douglas DC-2s bought for L.A.P.E. were faster than the Nieuport 52 fighters then in service with the *Aviación Militar*. It was then that Warleta decided to buy a series of fifty twin-engined Martin B-10 'Martin Bombers', whose construction under licence from the Glenn Martin company in the USA was envisaged by C.A.S.A. at Getafe. These aircraft, with their retractable landing gear, were very modern for the time. The choice of a fighter materialized in the Hawker Spanish Fury, fifty of which were to be built by La Hispano-Suiza under licence at Guadalajara. These were fixed landing gear biplane fighters, but it should be recalled that retractable landing gear monoplane fighters were still only at prototype stage at the time.

The *Aeronáutica Naval* also set about its modernization and chose the Hawker Osprey biplane for the *Escuadrilla de Combate y Acompañamiento* (Combat and Escort Squadron), to replace its obsolete Martinsyde F.4 fighters of First World War vintage. The ten Ospreys were to be built by C.A.S.A. at Getafe.

Teniente piloto Gutiérrez Lanzas and oficial 3º de Aeronáutica Naval Carlos Lázaro in front of a Vickers Vildebeest at Manises in Valencia, August 1936.

Breguet XIXs of Grupo de Reconocimiento Estratégico nº 31 at Getafe.

A Nieuport 52 of Grupo nº 11 refuelling at Getafe. The aircraft carries the red bands of the government forces. To the left is one of three modern Hawker Furies which equipped the government air force.

Below: Armourers of Grupo nº 31 at Getafe fit bomb racks on the lower wing of a Breguet XIX.

AIR WAR OVER SPAIN

THE SPANISH CIVIL WAR
Front lines July 1936
Nationalist
Republican

Spanish aviation in 1936

In July 1936 Spanish aviation, both civil and military, depended on the *Dirección General de Aeronáutica*, at the time an organ of the *Ministerio de la Guerra*, and under the command of *general de división* Miguel Núñez de Prado.

The February 1936 elections, which brought the left wing parties back to power in a wide Popular Front coalition, involved a convulsive period of revanchism. The new government, with Santiago Casares Quiroga as president, made no substantial changes in aviation, but it did affect personnel policy. As mentioned earlier, it was the previous government which had decided to buy new air equipment, but its arrival, which started in December 1935 in the form of three new twin-engined military version De Havilland DH-89 Dragon Rapides, fitted with bomb racks and machine guns, and De Havilland DH-82 Tiger Moth trainers, was not completed until June 1936. In this period the three first Hawker Spanish Fury fighters arrived in Spain to be used as patterns for the series to be built by La Hispano-Suiza at Guadalajara. There was no time to wait for the arrival of the Martin B-10 bombers.

In fact, in July 1936 there were about 360 aircraft in Spain suitable for military use, of which some 300 were single-engined and the rest were multi-engined aircraft. Half of these aircraft were reconnaissance light bomber Breguet-XIX sesquiplanes, a quarter of them were Nieuport 52 C1 fighters and the rest were *Aeronáutica Naval* aircraft, which also had ground aircraft similar to the military Breguet XIXs, the Vickers Vildebeest torpedo aircraft, and biplane Savoia S.62 seaplanes. About 60 per cent of the multi-engined aircraft were Dornier *Wal* flying boats, nearly all of them temporarily grounded by a problem with the engine reducers, while of the remaining twenty-four, the best were the Fokker F.VII 3ms and Douglas DC-2s.

The right wing rebels had nearly half of the Breguet XIXs at the León, Logroño, Seville and Africa air bases; nine Dornier *Wal* flying boats in Africa and Pollensa; five Savoia-62s at Marín, Pontevedra; three military Fokker F.VII 3ms in Seville and Africa, and a Douglas DC-2 – although there was not a single operational fighter, they would soon have three Nieuport 52 C1s that landed in error at Armilla air base, Granada and another one which changed sides from Madrid to Burgos and some others which were gradually finishing overhaul at the *Parque Sur de Aviación* (South Aviation Maintenance Park) at Tablada, Seville. This made a total of about 100 aircraft available to the rebels.

The government had more than half of the Breguet XIXs of *Grupo nº 31* and all of the Nieuport 52 C1s of *Grupos de caza nº 11* at Getafe with *nº 13* in Barcelona, while the Fokker F.VII 3ms and

8

THE SPANISH SECOND REPUBLIC AND AVIATION

A Dornier Do J Wal of the Aeronáutica Naval flies over the Columbretes Islands in the Mediterranean.

Three military De Havilland DH 89 M Dragon Rapides arrived in Spain before the outbreak of the civil war. General Núñez de Prado was flown on this particular aircraft to Saragossa, where he was imprisoned.

CASA built 27 Vickers Vildebeest torpedo-bombers for the Aeronáutica Naval. All of them remained on the Republican side throughout the conflict.

The pilot of a Vickers Vildebeest climbs out of his aircraft at El Prat de Llobregat air base, Barcelona in late July 1936.

AIR WAR OVER SPAIN

A Nieuport is prepared for take-off at Getafe.

The pilot and observer about to board their Breguet XIX of Grupo nº 31 at Getafe in July 1936. Note the bomb racks fitted beneath the wing.

Right: Government ground crew prepare a Nieuport for another sortie.

Right: Comandante Hidalgo de Cisneros, the future commander of Republican aviation, flew Nieuport fighters at the start of the conflict and is seen here walking past such a machine.

Nieuport 52 coded 11-1 of Grupo nº 11 at Getafe. Note the Black Panther emblem on the tailfin.

L.A.P.E. Douglas DC-2s and all training aircraft were at Cuatro Vientos, Los Alcázares and Alcalá de Henares. Most of the *Aeronáutica Naval* aircraft, the twenty-seven Vickers Vildebeests, seven Dornier *Wal* and nearly thirty Savoia S-62 seaplanes, twelve old Martinsyde F.4 fighters and seven Hispano E.30 trainers, remained loyal to the government at the San Javier, Barcelona and Mahón bases.

The Breguet XIXs had been phased in with the *Aviación Militar* in 1925, and had seen their baptism of fire during the landing at Alhucemas, the Spanish protectorate in Morocco. The Breguet had also made the newspapers with the Madrid-Manila record flight. It was one of the best aircraft of the late 1920s, but in 1936 it was clearly overshadowed by other models. Normally it carried an ordnance of 12 kg bombs but it could carry 50 kg bombs, the latter being used during the Civil War.

The Dornier *Wal* had also been the most remarkable seaplane of its time, whereas the Fokker F.VII 3m trimotor was the first successful civil transport aircraft in the world.

Paradoxically and in military terms, the Douglas DC-2 was the most valuable aircraft in Spain, faster than any type including the Nieuport 52 C1 fighters. During the early months of the war both sides used them as makeshift bombers, fitting them with defensive armament.

As for military pilots in Spain, some 215 (38 per cent) chose to side with the Republic Government and around 175 (30 per cent) rebelled, whereas the rest, about 185 (32 per cent), were neutral and did not serve either side.

The central aeronautical organs, such as the *Dirección General de Aeronáutica*, the *Oficina de Mando*

THE SPANISH SECOND REPUBLIC AND AVIATION

Dewoitine D-510TH, coded CW-002, flown by sargento José Sarrió Calatayud, Grupo Mixto nº 71 de Defensa de Costas

(Headquarters) and the *Jefaturas de Aviación* (Aviation Command Offices), remained loyal to the Madrid authorities. As regards territorial scope, out of the four large units, the three *Escuadras Aéreas* and the *Fuerzas Aéreas de África*, the main core of the *1ª Escuadra* in Madrid and the *3ª Escuadra* in Barcelona, proved loyal to the government, whereas the *2ª Escuadra* in Seville and the *Fuerzas Aéreas de África* in Tetuán, joined the rebels, as did the *Grupos de Reconocimiento Divisionarios nº 21* in León and *nº 23* in Logroño, which then became part of a new body called *Fuerzas Aéreas del Norte*. The *Servicio de Instrucción y Material* (Training and Materiel Service), the *Aeronáutica Naval* and L.A.P.E. also remained loyal to the government and elements of them formed the basis of the *2ª Escuadra*, based at Los Alcázares, Murcia while part of their air equipment served to reinforce the *1ª* and *3ª Escuadras*. The *2ª Escuadra* in Seville and the *Fuerzas Aéreas de África* remained under a single high command, which was entrusted to *general* Alfredo Kindelán, who was appointed chief of the Nationalist *Servicios del Aire*.

The fighting sides align

Essentially, modifications to Spanish aviation were limited to policies in personnel and organization. Shortly after the advent of the Popular Front, following the February 1936 elections, important changes took place in the *Jefatura de Aviación Militar*, which was an organ of the War Ministry. The Prime Minister, Santiago Casares Quiroga, who was also War Minister, upon advice from his aide, *comandante de Aviación* Ignacio Hidalgo de Cisneros – although not without some reticence – initiated important changes in command at air bases and headquarters units. He also dismissed a large number of senior and junior right-wing *Aviación* officers who were seen as potentially dangerous, and who were posted back to their original corps.

In this way Casares Quiroga tried to control the loyalty of the *Aviación Militar* commanders as much as possible and to have at his disposal the largest number of aircraft in case of a feared coup.

The general director of *Aeronáutica*, *general* Miguel Núñez de Prado, who had a sound Republican record and was a close collaborator of Casares Quiroga, supported this purge of the *Aviación* cadres. There are many testimonies regarding the steps taken in order to suppress any coup attempt and the

Ground crew posing in front of an escuadrilla of Nieuport 52s of Grupo nº 11.

Government ground crew assemble around a Nieuport 52 as it takes on fuel from a bowser.

11

AIR WAR OVER SPAIN

Watched by his ground crew, the pilot of a Nieuport 52 of Grupo nº 11 adjusts his parachute prior to take-off for another mission over the front.

purge of right-wing *Aviación* officers, such as *teniente coronel* Luis Romero Basart, then chief of *Aviación* liaison at the *2ª Inspección General del Ejército* in Madrid, or the above-mentioned *comandante* Ignacio Hidalgo de Cisneros.

The former wrote about the preparations for the organization of peoples' armed militias, to be made up of workers employed in *Aviación Militar* facilities. According to Romero Basart, *general* Núñez del Prado ordered pilot *capitán* José de la Roquette, then posted to the *Oficina de Mando de Aviación*, to create a workers' battalion at the Cuatro Vientos Workshops, which was to be armed with the rifles at the air base and those stored at the *Parque de Artillería* in Madrid, which had a right-wing commanding officer. A few days later, Núñez de Prado met the general directors of the *Guardia Civil* and the *Marina Mercante*, two generals and aviation *capitanes* Carlos Núñez Maza, technical secretary of the *Dirección General de Aeronáutica*, the above-mentioned José de la Roquette and Arturo González Gil de Santibáñez, director of the Aeronáutica Industrial S.A. (A.I.S.A.) aircraft factory at Carabanchel, as well as the pilot *teniente* Joaquín Mellado Pascual, interim director of L.A.P.E. The last two officers were retired by Azaña's law. Although Casares Quiroga disapproved of the meeting, that was no obstacle for the preparations regarding the aviation workers which continued developing in the same way.

Comandante Hidalgo de Cisneros recalled in his memoirs an episode regarding the storage of aviation equipment at the air bases trusted by the government and the neutralization of airmen engaged in the coup preparations. One day, shortly before the military uprising, Ramón Pruñorosa, the commanding officer of the Alcalá de Henares air base, home of the *Escuela de Vuelo y Combate*, went to his quarters to report that *comandante* Rafael Gómez Jordana and his officers were storing machine guns, ammunition and bombs, and had fitted bomb racks to the two Fokker F.VII 3ms and the three De Havilland DH-89 M Dragon Rapides that were used to train pilots on multi-engined aircraft. Hidalgo quickly reported to *general* Núñez de Prado and the latter, without even reporting to the War Minister, gave him written orders to take charge of the aircraft and armament stored at Alcalá. At once, *comandante* Hidalgo de Cisneros went to the Getafe air base, where a trusted group of senior and junior officers were gathering. There he met *capitanes* Manuel Cascón Briega, Avertano González Fernández and junior officers, Fernando Hernández Franch and Pedro Mansilla Martínez

The government-operated militarised LAPE Fokker F-VII 3m trimotor nº 16 registered EC-UAA. Note the red band on the fuselage.

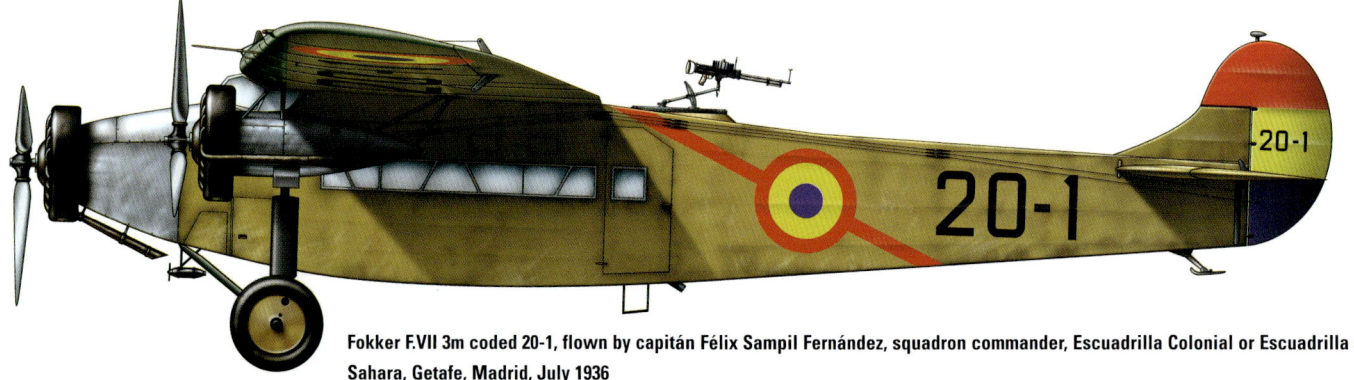

Fokker F.VII 3m coded 20-1, flown by capitán Félix Sampil Fernández, squadron commander, Escuadrilla Colonial or Escuadrilla del Sahara, Getafe, Madrid, July 1936

This trimotor, coded '20-1', was the original Dutch-manufactured aircraft that was used as a pattern for the licence construction of another three military F.VII 3m bombers at the Loring factory at Carabanchel.

THE SPANISH SECOND REPUBLIC AND AVIATION

A Patrulla of Breguet XIXs of Grupo nº 31 seen at Sariñena air base in August 1936.

Comandante Alfonso de los Reyes, commander of the Sariñena air base, in discussion with a group of milicianos on the airfield.

Sariñena airfield, August 1936: left, in white overalls, is alférez piloto Rodolfo Robles; centre, wearing goggles, teniente coronel Díaz Sandino, Jefe de la 3ª Región Aérea and right, comandante Alfonso de los Reyes, the air base commander.

An armourer sets the fuse on a 10 kg bomb at Sariñena air base in August 1936.

and went with them to Alcalá by car. There they found the only the officer of the day who, highly surprised, watched these officers load the weapons on board the multi-engined aircraft and take off for Getafe, where they landed without trouble. Once the mission was accomplished, Núñez de Prado and Hidalgo de Cisneros reported to Casares Quiroga, who was asked to disband the group of instructors at the *Escuela* at Alcalá. Very impressed with the proceedings, Casares Quiroga agreed with the request, but stated he would not act without consulting the President of the Republic, Manuel Azaña. On the following day, at the presidential palace at El Pardo, upon hearing of Casares Quiroga's detailed report, Azaña, still not believing it, prevented the War Minister from issuing the order to disband the group of instructors at the *Escuela*.

However, Casares Quiroga continued with his personnel policy, and issued an order to assign the *Aviación Militar* postings according to ministerial designation and not, as customary, according to seniority or competition. Thus, almost all cadres were replaced at the *Oficina de Mando de Aviación*, which was at the War Ministry and formed the real staff. Furthermore, the senior and junior officers who displayed the greatest Republican loyalty were chosen for the command of the main air bases and aviation organs; in general, as we shall see, this policy was quite efficient. The truth is that when the July 1936 coup took place, out of all the air base commanders, only two – *comandantes* Julián Rubio López at León and Roberto White Santiago at Logroño – gladly joined the military uprising, although both had enjoyed the full confidence of Casares Quiroga. The rest of the senior officers remained loyal to the Republic government, although three of them, two in the North Africa air bases – *comandante* Ricardo de la Puente Bahamonde and *capitán* Virgilio Leret Ruiz[2] – and one in Seville – *comandante* Rafael Martínez Esteve – were arrested by the rebels, along with some of their subordinates, because they opposed the rebels' plans.

As regards the *Aviación* plotters, they drew up a detailed plan to capture the air bases where they were posted, by storing arms and ammunition but, as will be revealed, they were somewhat over-optimistic in their attitude.

[2.] This officer had patented one of the first jet engines in the world.

AIR WAR OVER SPAIN

NCOs of the Aviación Militar pose in front of a Breguet XIX coded 12-24.

While the pilot of this Republican Breguet XIX checks his instruments, the observer studies a map of the flight route.

A Republican de Havilland DH-60 Moth light aircraft after a local 'overhaul' in Spain.

THE SPANISH SECOND REPUBLIC AND AVIATION

Comandante Hidalgo de Cisneros, the deputy commander of Escuadra nº 1, climbs out of Nieuport 52 coded 11-2 at Getafe.

The instructors and student pilots of the Republican Escuela de Vuelo Nocturno (Night Flight School) established at El Carmoli in Murcia. The aircraft in the background is a Koolhoven FK.51.

AIR WAR OVER SPAIN

Romeo Ro 41s were soon taken on by the Nationalists. Seen here is an Escuelas de Vuelo machine, '7-21'. ('Canario' Azaola)

This government Dragon Rapide is adorned with wide red government bands on its fuselage and wings.

CHAPTER TWO
THE OUTBREAK OF THE SPANISH CIVIL WAR

The failure of the military uprising at the Madrid, Barcelona and Murcia air bases

ON 18 July 1936 the best-equipped *Aviación Militar* air units were at the Getafe, Cuatro Vientos and Alcalá de Henares air bases in Madrid. Based there were the *1ª Escuadra de Aviación*, the *Escuela de Observadores*, service units and the *Escuela de Vuelo y Combate*. The commanding officers of the first two air bases, *tenientes coroneles* Antonio Camacho Benítez and Francisco León Trejo, were faithful defenders of Republican authority, whereas the third, *comandante* Rafael Gómez Jordana de Sousa, who was with the rebels, was not in Madrid at the time of the coup, but on summer leave. Camacho Benítez and León Trejo, with decisiveness and energy, managed to neutralize the group of officers, NCOs and a few other individuals, who were involved in the military uprising, either by expelling them from the air base or by sending them home as detainees, thus stopping them from taking any decisive action for the coup.

Thus, in the Spanish capital, it was the government aircraft that bombed the barracks of the rebel *Ejército de Tierra* units at Carabanchel, La Montaña, Getafe and Leganés, consequently preventing the rebel forces taking to the streets of Madrid and seizing the administrative and communication areas. In conjunction with these air strikes, the peoples' armed militias or the police forces loyal to the government eventually managed to enter the barracks and capture the rebels.

One of the rebel officers at the Getafe air base, the then *capitán piloto ingeniero aeronáutico* José Gomá Orduña, offered a very accurate description of the decisive action of the government aviation in Madrid to crush the coup. Gomá states that the situation facing a quartered garrison, standing alone for hours, even days, waiting for other forces to arrive and act together, was utter suicide. He recalls that even without the arrival of the expected reinforcements, if rebel airmen had flown aircraft over Madrid, the troops would have eventually poured into the streets. He wrote: 'Immediately after the flights over La Montaña barracks, disaster struck. The role of aviation was decisive. One has to admit that, even though with aviation deployed against them, if the [rebel] ground forces had launched an assault, Madrid would not have remained red, because the aviation would have not stopped an attack by dropping 10-kilogram bombs. But aviation simply had the threat of stopping the plan, thus gaining Madrid for the Republic.'

Soldiers of the Guardias de Asalto run past Breguet XIXs at Getafe during the uprising there or shortly after it was suppressed. Airmen and these soldiers protected Getafe air base after the coup by the Madrid garrison.

AIR WAR OVER SPAIN

The crew of one of the Escuadrilla 'España' Potez 540s pose in front of their aircraft at Barajas air base, Madrid. Left to right: Bernier, Steff, Dutetre, Guidez, Barcaiztegui and unknown.

Teniente coronel Díaz Sandino talks to anarchist leader García Oliver (later a minister) and other Republican leaders.

Summing up, Gomá admits that the aviation support to ground troops, under these circumstances, was of a psychological nature rather than an effective one, as the 50 kg bombs were the heaviest bombs dropped by the government aircraft, both by the military and civil Fokkers and the Dragon Rapides. But for a direct hit, the Hispania 10 kg bombs were practically useless.

The fourth air base in Madrid, Barajas airport, from where the L.A.P.E. Douglas DC-2s, Fokker F.VII 3ms and Ford F.5s operated, also saw important and dramatic events. The DC-2s, the most modern and fastest aircraft in Spain at the time which out-paced the *Aviación Militar* Nieuport 52 standard fighters, were immediately militarized and fitted with bombsights and even defensive machine gun positions, to be fired through the side windows. Most of the company's pilots, led by *teniente* Joaquín Mellado Pascual, were retired military pilots, supernumeraries or reserve pilots and therefore all of them experienced in the military use of transport aircraft.

These civil aircraft, once militarised by the Republican government, carried out important long-range bombing sorties on the rebel air bases in North Africa, Seville, León or Logroño, as well as liaison flights to the northern coast of Spain, landing in Asturias and Santander.

In Catalonia, the command of the *3ª Escuadra de Aviación* was at El Prat de Llobregat air base in Barcelona, where the commanding officer was *teniente coronel* Felipe Díaz Sandino, a senior officer with a sound Republican record. *Grupo de caza nº 13*, with a single Nieuport 52 *escuadrilla*, was based there with about six Breguet XIX reconnaissance aircraft of the *escuadra* staff. Díaz Sandino neutralised his second-in-command, *comandante* Castro Garnica, and some other officers who supported the coup, and allowed the popular militias entry into the base. These militias were under the command of retired infantry *comandante* Alfonso de los Reyes González de Cárdenas, whom Díaz Sandino appointed second-in-command of the base. With the few Breguet XIXs serviceable, they bombed the barracks of the rebel forces, and this contributed to their prompt surrender.

In Barcelona there were other air facilities and units, in this case those of the *Aeronáutica Naval* – the *Escuela de Aeronáutica* and the aero naval Workshops. Both facilities were located on the quayside at Contradique. The regular officers of the *Cuerpo General de la Armada* were all in favour of the coup and for that reason they allowed the arrival at the base, by air, of *general* Manuel Goded Llopis, who had been posted there to command the rebel forces in Barcelona. This general, who was in Palma de Majorca, left the Mahón naval air station for the capital of Catalonia on a Savoia S-62 seaplane and

Nieuport 52s of Grupo de Caza nº 13 lined up at El Prat de Llobregat, Barcelona. Note the four-leaf clover emblem on the tail fin of the aircraft in the foreground.

THE OUTBREAK OF THE SPANISH CIVIL WAR

Officers of the Aviación and Ejército gather in front of the Nieuport 52s of Grupo nº 13.

An escuadrilla of Breguet XIXs flies over an escuadrilla of Nieuport 52s of Grupo nº 13, possibly at El Prat de Llobregat, Barcelona.

took command of the headquarters of the *4ª División Orgánica*. Once he had left the naval air station, the junior officers posted there arrested their seniors and took control. It was then that the *Escuadrilla Escuela* seaplanes, the Savoia S-62s, Macchi M-18s and Dornier *Wal* operated in close support with the *Aviación Militar* Breguet XIXs, until the capitulation of Goded's forces.

In south-east Spain, in the province of Murcia, there were two important bases on the shores of the Mar Menor. The oldest one, at Los Alcázares, belonged to the *Aviación Militar* and the land aircraft of the *Escuela de Tiro y Bombardeo Aéreo* – Breguet XIXs, Hispano E-30s and Nieuport 52s – were based there, along with the Dornier *Wal* seaplanes of the *Grupo de Hidroaviones nº 6*. Also at Los Alcázares was the *Parque Regional Sureste* which undertook aircraft repairs and overhaul in the Levante region. The commander of these forces was *comandante* Juan Ortiz Muñoz, who had been decorated

An Aviación Militar Dornier Do J Wal seaplane, coded W-25 and numbered '6-15', at Los Alcázares. This aircraft was the only one serviceable in the Republican zone at the start of the civil war.

Breguet XIX, Aviación del Norte, Reus, Tarragona, February 1937
This uncoded government Breguet XIX was one of those sent from Reus, Tarragona in February 1937 to reinforce the Aviación del Norte. It was seriously damaged in a forced-landing in France, while flown by capitán Juan Macho Juárez.

AIR WAR OVER SPAIN

A government airman tests out a new parachute on the safety of terra firma.

with the *Medalla Militar Individual*, and was also a sound Republican and, along with all his subordinates, remained loyal to the Republican government.

In the suburbs of Los Alcázares was the San Javier *Base Aeronaval*, of the *Aeronáutica Naval*. This was the most modern air base in Spain, for it had been opened shortly after the advent of the Republic. Most of the *Aviación Naval* units were based there including the *Escuadrilla de Combate* (Combat Squadron [Martinsyde F.4]), the *Escuadrilla de Bombardeo* (Bomb Squadron [Dornier *Wal*]), the *Flotilla de Reconocimiento* (Reconnaissance Squadron [Savoia S-62]) and the *Escuadrilla de Adiestramiento* (Training Squadron [Hispano E-30]). Workshops and auxiliary services, such as radio, photography and a parachute section were also at San Javier. All senior officers of the *Armada*, with the commanding officer leading, *capitán de corbeta* José de la Rocha Bustamante, supported the uprising. However, their passive attitude, in waiting for orders from above, meant that they showed no initiatives. Furthermore, they informed the *Aeronáutica Naval* junior officers about their subversive plans, but the latter openly opposed the coup. One of the junior officers, *alférez* Manuel Carcellé, left the base and reported to *comandante* Ortiz at Los Alcázares. Carcellé quickly arranged one column of *Aviación Militar* soldiers. Moving cross-country at dawn, they entered the naval air station and took it without a single shot being fired. The Los Alcázares aircraft flew over San Javier and dropped leaflets calling for the surrender of the seamen. All of the *Aeronáutica Naval* senior officers were arrested and sent to Cartagena, where they were delivered to the naval authorities. All of them were to die shortly afterwards, murdered in an uncontrolled retaliation action carried out by deck ratings.

Comandante Ortiz Muñoz took command of both air bases and appointed *capitán* José Melendreras Sierra, of the *Aviación Militar*, as commander of the San Javier base, although shortly afterwards he was succeeded by naval aviation officer Manuel Carcellé. All of the Mar Menor aircraft were used to consolidate the government dominion over the whole Levante region and especially contributed to suppress the coup at the Almería and Albacete garrisons. *Comandante* Ortiz also sent *capitán* Narciso Muñoz del Corral to Armilla air base in Granada to take over command there but as it was impossible to do so, the latter, accompanied by two subaltern officers, ordered three Breguet XIX aircraft to leave for Los Alcázares and the air base ground crew unit to abandon it for Motril and Almería, an order that was carried out by an aviation NCO. These *Aviación* ground forces also contributed to attaining the surrender of the provincial capital of Granada.

Success for the coup in Morocco, and at Seville, Logroño and León air bases
Although opposed by the chief of the *Fuerzas Aéreas de África*, *comandante* Ricardo de la Puente Bahamonde, a cousin of *general* Francisco Franco, the rebels in the Morocco protectorate managed to gain control of the Sania Ramel (Tetuán), Nador and El Atalayón (Melilla) and Aumara (Larache) air bases. In Tetuán the rebel artillery had to bombard the air base facilities and exchanged machine gun fire with the *Aviación* troops who were resisting them from the base buildings. The *Regulares* – colonial indigenous troops – took the *Aviación* senior and junior officers, NCOs and soldiers as prisoners and were stationed as an interim garrison at the base until personnel from other air bases they could trust came in. *Comandante* Antonio Llorente Solá took over command of the *Fuerzas Aéreas de África* and his predecessor was shot shortly afterwards.

At the seaplane base at El Atalayón, in Melilla, *capitán* Virgilio Leret Ruiz[1], along with two junior officers and several NCOs who resisted an assault by the *Regulares*, were taken prisoner and the officers shot. The land air base at Melilla, Nador, was also taken by indigenous troops without opposition by the commander and officers, although on the following day *capitán* Pérez del Camino, the airfield commander, landed with his Breguet XIX in French Morocco with an unidentified *sargento*, but they did not join the government side.

[1.] This officer had patented one of the first jet engines in the world.

20

THE OUTBREAK OF THE SPANISH CIVIL WAR

José Calderón Gaztelu

José Calderón Gaztelu (Pamplona, 1904 - 1937)

Capitán Gaztelu qualified as a pilot in 1925 and at the time of the uprising was posted to the *Grupo de Reconocimiento Divisionario nº 23* at Recajo air base, Logroño where he joined the rebels. He flew Breguets and Fokker F-VII 3ms in 1936, serving on the North Front. Upon the arrival of Junkers Ju 52s, he flew them as well and in 1937 was appointed commander of an *escuadrilla* of *comandante* Alfonso Carrillo Durán's *2º Grupo*.

As the eldest *capitán*, Calderón was the interim Group commanding officer during the battle of the Jarama in February 1937. At the time, government fighters were very active, with four I-16 and I-15 squadrons. As for the Nationalists, the Heinkel He 51s of J/88 of the *Legion Condor* had suffered heavy losses and were clearly overpowered by their opponents, whereas the Italian CR.32 pilots of the *Aviación Legionaria* were very reluctant to fly across the lines during bombing sorties. Only García Morato's Spanish *patrulla* dared.

On the night of 15 February 1937, *capitán* Calderón uttered his famous phrase: 'Tomorrow my group will bomb, no matter who might fall…'

This rang true the following day when he led his unit, flying Ju 52 '22-58', and was shot down by opposition fighters. Only the *oficial observador* and the *sargento mecánico* managed to bale out. They were taken prisoner but later exchanged. Calderón was awarded a posthumous *Cruz Laureada de San Fernando*.

One other of the Grupos de Reconocimiento Divisionario, nº 21 was at La Virgen del Camino air base in León, also equipped with Breguet XIXs. It was dependent on Escuadra de Aviación nº 1, with headquarters in Madrid. The Jefatura de Aviación at the War Ministry trusted the commander, comandante Julián Rubio López, who had taken part in the Republican attempt at Cuatro Vientos air base. It was for that reason that his unexpected alignment with the rebels was a nasty surprise in Madrid.

At the Larache air base there was almost no opposition, as the commander, *capitán* Fernando Martínez Mejías, joined the coup with his subordinates. Their aircraft reinforced the Tetuán air base.

Subordinated to the *Fuerzas Aéreas de África*, but stationed in the air bases in the Cabo Juby, Ifni and Sahara colonies, was the so-called *Escuadrilla del Sahara*, equipped with four military Fokker F.VII 3ms and some De Havilland DH-82 Tiger Moths. The unit commander, *capitán* Félix Sampil Fernández de Granda, was on leave in Madrid to where he had flown Fokker F.VII 3m, coded 20-1, for an engine change. The interim *escuadrilla* commander, *capitán* Luis Burguete Reparaz, received orders from the *Jefatura de Aviación Militar* to move his aircraft to Tablada air base in Seville to bomb the rebel air bases in North Africa. Burguete accomplished the order only in part, for he arrived in Seville with the only two trimotors available; *tenientes* Mario Ureña Jiménez Coronado and Alfredo Arija Valenzuela, piloting the third machine, disobeyed and landed at Larache air base.

In Seville, the commander of the *2ª Escuadra*, *comandante* Rafael Martínez Esteve, remained loyal to the government and allowed militarised L.A.P.E. Douglas DC-2s and Fokker F.VII 3ms to be fitted with bombsights, bomb racks and bombs, to attack the Tetuán and Melilla air bases and barracks. The aircraft led by *teniente* Joaquín Mellado, carried out their first and only sortie from Tablada air base, as the aircraft returned to Barajas in Madrid without a stop-over in Seville after the bombing raid.

At Seville air base there was a serious incident between *capitán* Carlos Martínez Vara de Rey and the L.A.P.E. crew, when the former fired a rifle on the engines of a Douglas DC-2. *Comandante* Martínez Esteve managed to control the situation momentarily, and got the wounded *capitán* Vara de Rey arrested, ordering a judiciary inquiry.

Shortly afterwards, *capitán* Luis Burguete's two Fokker F.VII 3m had arrived and he was ordered to fly a reconnaissance sortie over Seville, which he did, but he did not bomb the rebel troops who were now on the streets of the capital of Andalusia. *General* Queipo de Llano, who had assumed command of the *2ª División Orgánica*, urged Martínez Esteve over the telephone to resign as commander of the air base which he later agreed to do, also relieving command of his deputy, *comandante* Rogelio de Azaola Ondarza. Martínez Esteve was arrested by the rebels and was later court martialled, although he survived, and was sentenced to life imprisonment.

Recajo, Logroño was the base of *Grupo de Reconocimiento Divisionario nº 23*, of *Escuadra de Aviación nº 3*, equipped with Breguet XIXs, although only one *escuadrilla* was operational. The commanding officer, *comandante* Roberto White Santiago, along with several of his *capitanes*, anticipated events and potential opposition from some junior officers, especially a group of NCOs and mechanics and some NCOs loyal to the Madrid government, and put them on preventive detention as they were boarding the bus driving them from the capital of La Rioja to the air base. *Comandante* White allowed ground troops from the Logroño garrison to enter the air base and thus secured control over it. The Logroño Breguet XIXs moved to Saragossa air base and operated on the Aragon front.

AIR WAR OVER SPAIN

A patrulla of three Breguet XIXs of Grupo nº 23 take off from Recajo, Logroño.

Above left and above: Breguet XIXs of the Grupo de Reconocimiento nº 21 at Leon. Note the 'Lion with a Cold' emblem on the tail which alludes to the cold climate of the region. Leon means 'lion' in Spanish.

Republican ground crew work on Breguet XIXs at Leon.

Above: An excellent view of a Breguet XIX, coded 21-57, of Grupo nº 21 based at Leon.

The parking area at Leon crowded with the Breguet XIXs of Grupo nº 21.

22

THE OUTBREAK OF THE SPANISH CIVIL WAR

One other of the *Grupos de Reconocimiento Divisionarios, nº 21* was at La Virgen del Camino air base in León, also equipped with Breguet XIXs. It was dependent on *Escuadra de Aviación nº 1*, with headquarters in Madrid. The *Jefatura de Aviación* at the War Ministry trusted the commander, *comandante* Julián Rubio López, who had taken part in the Republican attempt at Cuatro Vientos air base. It was for that reason that his unexpected alignment with the rebels was a nasty surprise in Madrid.

Above: A Fiat CR.32 being assembled at Melilla. Note the upper wing still carries Italian tricolour markings, while the fuselage has the black circle of the Nationalist air force.

Top left: A Fiat CR.32 fuselage being unloaded at the port of Melilla.

A group of Italian and Spanish airmen with Regulares officers at Melilla air base.

The procurement of new air equipment

Both sides were soon attempting to obtain aircraft in foreign markets. The rebels headed primarily for Germany, Italy, Britain and Portugal, whereas the government purchasing commissions went to France and Britain, although they also gave a try to Berlin, obviously with no success.

In the Canary Islands, the rebels seized a LuftHansa Junkers Ju 52/3m trimotor, D-APOK, *Max von Müller*, flown by captain Alfred Henke. This aircraft was used to fly a political and military commission to Germany, which included *capitán ingeniero aeronáutico* Francisco Arranz Monasterio. This officer was carrying a request for transport and fighter aircraft, as well as a variety of armament from Germany. Many works have covered the different stages of the gestation of what was later called *Unternehmen Feuerzauber* (Operation *Magic Fire*), Germany's support to the rebels. Actually, the first German aircraft did not arrive until early August 1936. These were the twenty Junkers Ju 52/3m trimotors that were flown to Tetuán air base from the Dessau factory, with a stopover in Rome, and later six Heinkel He 51 fighters that were offloaded in the port of Cadiz on 6 August 1936.

However, the first imported military aircraft to arrive in rebel hands came from Italy. These aircraft were nine Savoia Marchetti SM.81 trimotors that landed at Nador air base, Melilla, on 30 July 1936. This expedition, which flew from Sardinia, was actually made up of twelve aircraft but three were lost, either crashing at sea or in landing accidents in Algeria. Subsequently six Fiat CR.32 fighters arrived in Melilla by sea, with aircrews, ground crews and spares on 14 August.

On the British market, Nationalist agents, including the engineer Juan de la Cierva y Codorniú, the inventor of the autogiro, managed to buy several De Havilland DH-89 Dragon Rapides in London, as well as some Dutch Fokker F.VII 3m and Fokker F.XII trimotors which had served with British airlines. The first De Havilland DH-89 arrived in Burgos on 1 August and bombed the Trubia arms factory in Asturias on the following day.

Additional aircraft arrived from Germany in the following months, including six Heinkel He 51s, two Junkers Ju 52s and twenty Heinkel He 46 parasol tactical reconnaissance monoplanes, delivered in August 1936.

In September, the German semi-covert organization dealing with the supply of aircraft to Spain, *Sonderstab* (Special Staff) '*W*' received requests for new orders, for delivery in October and November 1936. These covered:

23

AIR WAR OVER SPAIN

Excellent view of a De Havilland DH-89 Dragon Rapide of Grupo Mixto Dragon-Fokker. This aircraft, '40-1', was named 'Capitán Pouso'. One airman was killed flying this aircraft type in Spain. (Foto Felipe Ezquerro)

Spanish Nationalist troops preparing to board Ju 52/3ms early in the Civil War. Because the Spanish Navy had remained largely Republican, it was impossible for Franco to ferry his experienced Moorish troops from Morocco to Spain by sea. The solution came in the form of twenty Ju 52 and eleven S.81 transport aircraft donated by Germany and Italy respectively.

24 Heinkel He 51s, for Spanish forces

12 Heinkel He 51s, to reinforce the first German fighter *Staffel* in Spain under the command of *Oberleutnant* Kraft Eberhardt

3 Messerschmitt Bf 109 prototype fighters for tests

3 Junkers Ju 52s

1 Heinkel He 50, for tests

2 Henschel Hs 123s ('Stuka'), for tests with air and ground crews

As regards the aircraft purchasing arrangements made abroad by the Republican government, technical commissions of military aeronautical engineers were sent immediately to Paris, London and even Berlin. *Comandantes* Ismael Warleta de la Quintana and Juan Aboal went to the French capital and made a request at the French Air Ministry for bombers and fighters, as well as bombs. These arrangements materialized in fourteen Dewoitine D-372 parasol monoplane fighters and six Potez 540 twin-engined bombers that arrived at El Prat de Llobregat air base in Barcelona on 7 and 8 August 1936. These military aircraft were followed on 26 August by a seventh Potez bomber (544 version) and a Bloch MB 210 twin-engined bomber, and five gull-wing Loire 46 monoplane fighters which arrived in Spain on 5 and 7 September. All these French aircraft were sent to Spain minus armament but their machine guns were never delivered.

THE OUTBREAK OF THE SPANISH CIVIL WAR

With these deliveries, France had used up its permitted options for selling military aircraft and proposed the establishment of a policy of Non-Intervention in the war in Spain to European countries on 8 August, which was accepted by the totalitarian governments of Italy and Germany. In fact, aircraft deliveries from these countries to the rebels had already equalled or even exceeded those from the French.

The first foreign aircraft to arrive in Republican Spain were four Air France Latécoère 28 single-engined aircraft, which had landed at El Altet air base in Alicante by late July 1936. The government authorities immediately seized these aircraft, which had been sent by the French government to evacuate their citizens in view of the seriousness of the Spanish situation. This created a diplomatic incident between both countries which was solved with the secret purchase of the aircraft by the Spanish government. Despite the fact that these were civil aircraft, two of them, fitted with bomb racks at Los Alcázares air base, were used to bomb the rebel air base at Armilla, Granada by early August.

Aeronautical engineer *comandante* Carlos Pastor Kraüel also went to Britain on a government commission and managed to purchase several civil aircraft: three Monospar ST. 25s, one Miles Hawk, one Miles Falcon, six De Havilland DH-84 Dragons and DH-89 Dragon Rapides, two Airspeed AS.6 Envoys and one Airspeed AS.8 Viceroy. Another Airspeed Envoy had been sent to Paris by *comandante* Pastor and was ready to leave for Republican Spain from the French capital. Shortly before leaving the United Kingdom, Pastor had managed to purchase a further six De Havilland DH-89 Dragon Rapides and five Airspeeds AS.5 models. But the British government put an embargo on this total of eleven British aircraft and, although arduous diplomatic arrangements to send them to Spain were made, the aircraft never left Britain.

In September 1936 additional government aeronautical commissions were established. One of them went to the USA, Mexico and Canada, where they managed to purchase aircraft – mostly commercial types – for the Spanish Republic. This commission was made up of engineers Francisco León Trejo, José Melendreras and Francisco Corral. Further commissions were sent to Czechoslovakia and other central European countries. *Coronel* Ángel Pastor Velasco, the Air Under-Secretary, was arrested in Czechoslovakia holding false papers. However, he managed to purchase Letov Š.231 fighters and Aero A.101 light bomber aircraft.

However, the greatest supplier of military aviation equipment to the Spanish Republic was to be Soviet Russia.

Aircraft supplied to the Nationalist Forces (1936-1939)

GERMANY

Combat
Arado Ar 68 E	4
Arado Ar 95 A	3
Dornier Do 17 E, F, P	32
Heinkel He 45	45
Heinkel He 46 C	20
Heinkel He 50 G	1
Heinkel He 51 B, C	134
Heinkel He 59 B	27
Heinkel He 60 E	7
Heinkel He 70 E, F	28
Heinkel He 111 B, E	97
Heinkel He 112 V, B	17
Heinkel He 115 A	2
Henschel Hs 123 A	6
Henschel Hs 126 A	8
Junkers Ju 52/3m	67
Junkers Ju 86 D	5
Junkers Ju 87 V, A, B	13
Messerschmitt Bf 109 V, B, C, D, E	139

Transport, trainers, etc.
Arado Ar 66 C	6
Bücker Bü 131 A, B	55
Bücker Bü 133 C	21
Fieseler Fi 156 A	6
Gotha Go 145 A	21
Junkers W 34 hi	7
Junkers Ju 52/3m W	1
Klemm L.32 aXIV	4
Messerschmitt Bf 108 B	6

ITALY

Combat
Breda Ba.64	1
Breda Ba.65	23
Cant Z.501	10
Cant Z.506	4
Caproni Ca.135	2
Caproni Ca.310	10
Fiat BR.20	13
Fiat CR.32	377
Fiat G.50	10
Macchi M.41	3
Romeo Ro.37	68
Romeo Ro.41	28
Savoia Marchetti S.55X	3
Savoia Marchetti SM.81	84
Savoia Marchetti SM.79	90

Transport, trainers, etc.
Breda Ba.25	1
Breda Ba.28	6
Breda Ba.33	1
Breda Ba.39	1
Caproni Ca.100	2

Caproni AP.1	10
Fiat CR.20	6
Fiat CR.30	2

POLAND
Combat
PWS-10	20

Transport, trainers, etc.
RWD-13	4

BRITAIN
Transport, trainers, etc.
Airspeed AS.6 Envoy II	1
De Havilland DH-89 Dragon Rapide	4
Fokker F.VII/3m	2
Fokker F.XII	2

PORTUGAL
Transport, trainers, etc.
Farman F-191	1
Miles M.2 Hawk	1

FRANCE
Transport, trainers, etc.
Caudron C.272 Luciole	1
Caudron C.601 Aiglon	1
Fokker F.VII	1

CAPTURED ON ENEMY SHIPS
Combat
Aero A 101	22

Transport, trainers, etc.
Fairchild 91	1
Lockheed L.10 Electra	1
Northrop 1D Delta	2
Vultee V.1 A	4

Aircraft supplied to the Republican Aviación Militar (1936-1939)

SOVIET UNION
Combat
Polikarpov I-15 *Chato*	153
Polikarpov I-15bis *Superchato*	30
Polikarpov I-16 *Mosca*	276
Polikarpov R.5 *Rasante*	31
Polikarpov RZ *Natacha*	93
Tupolev SB *Katiuska*	93
Total combat	**676**

Transport, trainers, etc.
Polikarpov UTI-4 *Mosca*	4
Total transport, trainers, etc.	**4**

Subtotal **680**

FRANCE
Combat
Blériot Spad 51	1
Blériot Spad 91	1
Dewoitine D.371/372	18
Dewoitine D.510	2
Loire 46	5
Potez 540/542	14
Marcel Bloch 210	7 (5 knocked-down)
Breguet 460	1
Gourdou Lesseurre GL-32	16
Potez 25 A	5
Total combat	**70**

Transport, trainers, etc.
Beechcraft 17	1
Blériot Spad 56	1
Blériot Spad 111	2
Breguet 470	1
Caudron C.59	10
Caudron C.272/227 Luciole	10
Caudron C.600/601 Aiglon	25
Couzinet 101	1
Dewoitine D.27/53	2
Farman F.190/197	7
Farman F-401/402	5
Farman F.430/431/4322	4
Farman F.481	12
Hanriot H.437/439	7
Latécoère 28	4
Maillet 20/21	2
Morane Saulnier MS.181	4
Morane Saulnier MS.230	3
Morane Saulnier MS.341	3
Moreau 10	1
Potez 36/43	2
Potez 56	4
Romano R.82	6
SAB SEMA 12	1
Total transport, trainers, etc.	**118**

Subtotal **188**

CZECHOSLOVAKIA
Combat
Aero A.101	6
Letov Š.231	17
Total combat	**23**

Transport, trainers, etc.
Avia 51	3
Total transport, trainers, etc.	**3**

Subtotal **26**

ESTONIA
Combat
Bristol Bulldog	8
Potez 25	8
Total combat	16

Subtotal **16**

THE OUTBREAK OF THE SPANISH CIVIL WAR

USA
Combat
Seversky SEV 3	1
Vultee V. 1/V.1A	8
Northrop 2/5 Gamma	2
Total combat	**11**

Transport, trainers, etc.
Consolidated 20A Fleetster	2
Douglas DC-2	1
Lockheed Vega	1
Lockheed Sirius	1
Lockheed Orion	3
Northrop Delta	1
Spartan 7 Executive	3
Total transport, trainers, etc.	**12**

Subtotal — **25**

CANADA
Combat
Grumman GE. 23 *Delfín*	34
Total combat	**34**

Subtotal — **34**

HOLLAND
Combat
Fokker C.X	1
Fokker D.XXI	1
Koolhoven FK.51	22
Total combat	**24**

Transport, trainers, etc.
Fokker F.VII	1
Fokker F.IX	1
Fokker F.XII	1
Fokker F.XVIII	1
Fokker F.XX	1
Koolhoven FK.40	1
Total transport, trainers, etc.	**6**

Subtotal — **30**

SWITZERLAND
Transport, trainers, etc.
Douglas DC-2	1
Clark GA 43A	1
Lockheed 9B Orion	2
Total transport, trainers, etc.	**4**

Subtotal — **4**

SWEDEN
Transport, trainers, etc.
Sikorski S 38B	1
Northrop 1C Delta	1
Total transport, trainers, etc.	**2**

Subtotal — **2**

BRITAIN
Transport, trainers, etc.
Airspeed AS.6 Envoy	9
Airspeed AS.8 Viceroy	1
Avro 626 Cadet	1
Avro 643 Tutor	1
Bellanca 28/70	1
De Havilland DH-84 Dragon	4
De Havilland DH-82 Tiger Moth	12
De Havilland DH-89 Dragon Rapide	12
De Havilland DH-90 Dragonfly	3
Douglas DC-1	1
Focke Wulf Fw 56 Stösser	3
G.A. Monospar ST12/25	10
Miles M.2 Hawk	4
Miles M.3 Falcon	1
Percival Gull	1
Spartan Cruiser	1
Total transport, trainers, etc.	**66**

Subtotal — **66**

Aircraft built in Spain during the War

Combat
Polikarpov I-15 *Chato*	237
Polikarpov I-16 *Mosca*	10
Savoia S.62	4
Total combat	**251**

Transport, trainers, etc.
Gil Pazó GP.1	40
Hispano E-30	20
Hispano E-34	5
Total transport, trainers, etc.	**65**

Subtotal — **316**

Total (by country)
Soviet Union	680
France	188
Czechoslovakia	26
Estonia	16
USA	25
Canada	34
Holland	30
Switzerland	4
Sweden	2
Britain	66
Built in Spain	316
Total	**1,387**

AIR WAR OVER SPAIN

Dewoitine D.372 '12' flown by volunteer French capitaine Victor Veniel, seen here smiling and saluting from the cockpit with a raised fist.

The Fiat CR.32 carries the slogan 'Monico, presente' on its fuselage, intended to honour the Italian tenente shot down and killed on 31 August 1936.

This Fiat CR.32 has force-landed in open Spanish countryside during the summer of 1936.

Several Miles light aircraft, such as the Hawk seen here, were bought on the British market for Republican flying schools.

THE OUTBREAK OF THE SPANISH CIVIL WAR

This single government Airspeed AS-8 Viceroy was used in the bombing, transport and training roles. This photograph shows the aircraft at Celrá air base in Gerona in April 1937.

A rare view of the only Miles Sparrowhawk light aircraft to see service in Spain, coded '5' on its tail fin and wearing the red bands of the Republican aviation.

AIR WAR OVER SPAIN

An unidentified Republican sargento piloto in a typical period portrait. He is wearing a dress cap with white cover and a leather flight jacket with a pilot badge on his chest.

Czech Letov S-231 fighters were used for coastal defence by the Republican Grupo nº 71. (J. Salas)

The Junkers W 34 was used by the Nationalists for meteorological, transport and liaison duties. (Salgado)

Right: This Airspeed AS.6 Envoy was used to transport the Portuguese military mission on its tour of Nationalist Spain. Notice the unusually wide St Andrew's cross.

30

THE OUTBREAK OF THE SPANISH CIVIL WAR

A Miles M.2 light aircraft carrying the civil registration CS-AAL and markings of the Nationalist Aviación Militar. Its owner, the Portuguese volunteer Pequito Rebello, stands by his aircraft for this photograph.

Breda Ba 65s, such as '16-23', were used in the assault role by the Nationalists. ('Canario' Azaola)

Breda Ba.65, coded 16-12, 65ª Squadriglia Assalto, 35º Grupo Autonomo Misto
This aircraft survived the civil war and became part of the post-war Ejército del Aire.

AIR WAR OVER SPAIN

Fiat BR. 20s were used by the Italian Grupo Mixto, along with Ba 65s. Here, BR.20 '23-21' flies with a Savoia S.79. ('Canario' Azaola)

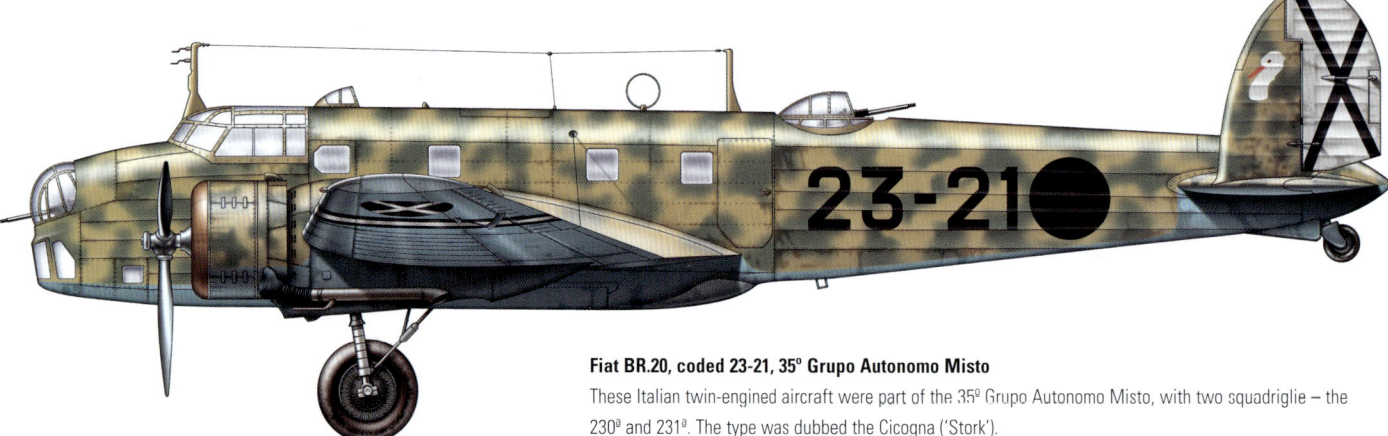

Fiat BR.20, coded 23-21, 35º Grupo Autonomo Misto
These Italian twin-engined aircraft were part of the 35º Grupo Autonomo Misto, with two squadriglie – the 230ª and 231ª. The type was dubbed the Cicogna ('Stork').

The importance of the air bridge over the Straits

The first air bridge in history was conceived on 20 July 1936 in a very original and quite spontaneous way at the Tetuán air base during the early days of the civil war following a meeting of senior officers held at the Moroccan base headed by *general* Franco.

The *Aviación* senior officers of the protectorate displayed great imagination and courage when suggesting the possibility of using the three colonial Fokker F.VII 3ms to take on the transfer of the *Ejército de África* to the peninsula by air, something never thought of before. The commanders' board accepted the proposal at once.

The air bridge commenced the very same day, the three military Fokker F.VIIs flying from the Sania Ramel/Tetuán and Tablada/Seville air bases. Two *Aeronáutica Naval* Dornier *Wal* seaplanes joined in the task from the beginning, making flights between the ports of Ceuta and Algeciras (Cadiz), and a L.A.P.E. Douglas DC-2 also joined in on 25 July, all of them flown by Spanish pilots. Many of the airmen in North Africa and Seville competed to get involved as co-pilots, and thus the air bridge also became, in effect, a multi-engined aircraft school.

From 20-28 July 1936, the *4ª* and *5ª Banderas* of the *Tercio* were moved to Seville at an an average of 120 legionnaires a day. The Fokker F.VII 3ms took it in turns to fly troops and carry out night-bombing and reconnaissance sorties, as far as Albacete and Madrid. Pilots slept in turns in the cockpits or in the brief breaks between sorties.

On 29 July, the new Jerez de la Frontera air base at Cadiz was readied, which substantially improved the flights, and the first German Junkers Ju 52 trimotor joined the air bridge, although flown by Spanish pilots at this time. This allowed an increase in the load and frequency of flights, 241 soldiers, for example being carried on the 30th.

In seventeen days, from 19 July to 4 August 1936, eight assault battalions were moved from Africa to the Peninsula, six of which were flown in, the other two being moved by sea, which represented nearly 40 per cent of the battalion strength in the Spanish Protectorate in Morocco.

Oddly enough, the government air force command did not issue orders to attack the air bridge aircraft, despite messages sent to Madrid by the air base commander at El Rompedizo, *teniente* Aurelio Villimar.

THE OUTBREAK OF THE SPANISH CIVIL WAR

A Romeo Ro.37 reconnaissance aircraft/light bomber, coded 12-20, on patrol over mountainous terrain.

The Nationalists captured twenty-two Czech Aero A 101s on board the SS Hordena in the Bay of Biscay.

A Lockheed L-10 Electra captured on board the SS Mar Cantábrico. This aircraft was used by General Alfredo Kindelán, Commander-in-Chief of the Nationalist air arm.

Grumman GE.23 'Delfín' coded CD-016 / White '1', teniente Nicomedes Calvo Aguilar and sargento Observador Cándido Maderuelo de la Cruz, 1ª Escuadrilla, Grupo Mixto nº 71 de Defensa de Costas

The Canadian-made Grumman GE.23 Delfín (Dolphin) biplanes equipped the Grupo nº 28 of the Spanish Republic, with two escuadrillas. Towards the end of the war, they were assigned to Grupo Mixto nº 71 de Defensa de Costas.

The *Aviación del Tercio*

Shortly after their arrival in Spain, the first twelve Italian Fiat CR.32 fighters were supplemented by a further nine which were landed in Vigo and then moved by rail to the Tablada air base at Seville, where they were assembled. Also, some time later, Romeo Ro.37 reconnaissance and light bomber aircraft arrived and these formed two squadrons, into which Spanish airmen were incorporated.

Tenente colonnello Ruggero Bonomi, who had commanded the first Savoia SM.81 expedition and had been promoted one rank, was appointed commander of the *Aviación del Tercio*[2] during the days that followed. He set about the organization of the air forces under his command, as follows:

Early Composition of the Italian *Aviación Del Tercio*

***Aviación del Tercio* Commander**: *tenente colonnello* Ruggero Bonomi
Second-in-Command: *maggiore* Altomare
Aide: *tenente* Erasi

[2.] The current *Legión española* was established in 1920 under the designation *Tercio de extranjeros*, following the model of the French *Légion Étrangère*, and was intended as a shock troop for the colonial war in Morocco. It was reorganized in 1937 and the current name was adopted. During the civil war, the Italian aviation, made up of foreign troops, was in theory a part of the *Tercio*, hence the sobriquet *Aviación legionaria* or *Aviazione Legionaria*.

AIR WAR OVER SPAIN

Ju 87 Stukas saw their operational debut in Spain in December 1937 but were used exclusively by the Legion Condor. This particular Ju 87 A-1, coded 29-4, belonged originally to St.G 163 and, together with the Ju 87s Bs, was flown by a large number of personnel in order to provide as many crews as possible with combat experience. All of them were returned to Germany after the war. The photograph depicts Junkers Ju 87 A '29-4'. (Calparsoro)

Junkers Ju 87 A-1, coded 29-2, 5.J./88, Legion Condor
The first Ju 87 operational unit made its debut during the Teruel operations in February 1938 as part of the Stuka Kette, or 5.J./88, of the Legion Condor. This aircraft was the usual machine of the crew comprised of Unteroffizieren Ernst Bartels (pilot) and Alfred Fleisch (radio operator).

Grupo Savoia SM.81
CO: *tenente colonnello* Allio
1ª Escuadrilla: *Capitano* Spotti
2ª Escuadrilla: *Capitano* Salvetat
3ª Escuadrilla: *Capitano* Muti

Escuadrilla de Caza Fiat CR.32
CO: *Capitano* Dequal

Imported German and Italian equipment takes the lead

Although numerical superiority of its aircraft in the early days of the war seemed to tip the balance of air superiority in the government's favour, it is nevertheless true that the lack of perspective of the *Oficina de Mando de Aviación* officers in Madrid prevented a crushing victory by Republican fighter pilots over the rebel air assets.

The dispersion of the Nieuport 52 fighter squadrons, sent in two- or three-aircraft patrols to a range of advanced airstrips, or the repeated and useless vigilance missions over the Sierra in Madrid, soon caused an important depreciation in government aircraft.

Although the arrival of six German Heinkel He 51 and twelve Italian Fiat CR.32 fighters for the Nationalists in August did not seem to change the situation substantially, the truth is that the Heinkel He 51s managed to score notable successes in their early operations on the Sierra front by shooting down several enemy Breguet XIXs, Nieuport 52s and Potez 540s. By late August, the Italian CR.32 fighters arrived on the central front, although two of them were shot down early on in combat on the Extremadura front.

However, the Nationalist troops managed to capture Talavera de la Reina in the province of Toledo by early September 1936, which prompted a major political crisis that caused the fall of Giral's government.

In Madrid, the new government established by Socialist leader Francisco Largo Caballero, established the *Ministerio de Marina y Aire* and the *Subsecretaría del Aire*. Shortly afterwards, the rebels conferred supreme command to *general* Francisco Franco, who kept *general* Alfredo Kindelán as *Jefe del Aire*.

In September and October, in the light of the fact that the Fiat CR.32 fighters were out-performing and dominating the French Dewoitine D-372s and Loire 46s, facilitating the advance of

THE OUTBREAK OF THE SPANISH CIVIL WAR

Airspeed AS-6 Envoys registered to the French Air Pyrénées company, were used by the Basque government, their real owners. Two of these aircraft were shot down by Nationalist fighters. ('Canario' Azaola)

the African expeditionary forces on Toledo and the outskirts of Madrid, Largo Caballero, in order to ensure efficient military aid, shipped the Bank of Spain gold reserves to the Soviet Union.

The wear and tear upon the government aviation during this period was such that by late October 1936 there was only one fighter in service for the defence of Madrid: a lonely Hawker Spanish Fury, which soon suffered an accident and became unserviceable.

A change in air superiority: the Russians arrive
The Soviet Union was the first European country to supply first-class air equipment to the Spanish government. According to a document dated 20 December 1936 and signed by *teniente coronel* Ignacio Hidalgo de Cisneros, commander-in-chief of the Republican *Fuerzas Aéreas*, thirty Tupolev SB *Katiuskas*, thirty-one Polikarpov R.5 *Rasantes*, twenty-five Polikarpov I-15 *Chatos* and thirty-one Polikarpov I-16 *Moscas* had arrived from the Soviet Union by that date. Not mentioned were an additional fifteen Polikarpov I-15 *Chatos* that had arrived in the North.

The Tupolev SB *Katiuska* twin-engined bombers were in combat on 28 October 1936, whereas the Polikarpov I-15 *Chato* biplane fighters were so employed on 4 November and the excellent Polikarpov I-16 *Mosca* monoplanes on the 13th.

From the first moment, the presence of the 71 Russian aircraft with retractable landing gear – the Tupolev SB bombers and the Polikarpov I-16 fighters – had completely altered the terms in the air struggle in the skies over Spain. Neither the Italian Fiat CR.32 fighters nor German Heinkel He 51s were fast enough to maintain firing range, in horizontal flight, on the new enemy *Katiuska* bombers. The I-16 *Mosca* fighters, with their modern aerodynamics and retractable landing gear, out-paced the Fiats and the Heinkels and enjoyed a very superior ceiling over the Fiat CR.32 which could only give a good account of itself in its higher diving speed and manoeuvrability, which was, however, inferior to that of the Polikarpov I-15 *Chato*. The German Heinkel He 51 biplanes were beaten by all of them.

General Alfredo Kindelán tried to face the challenge of the Russian aircraft by increasing to three the only Fiat CR.32 *escuadrilla* existing thus far and the one hundred aircraft of the recently arrived German air contingent in Spain, the *Legion Condor*, whose numerical potential was slightly inferior to that of the Soviet air expeditionary corps. But the disadvantage in quality was such that these aircraft were clearly inferior to the modern Polikarpov I-16 and Tupolev SB. Only the single-

Heinkel He 111 E-1, coded 25-45, K./88, Legion Condor
The Legion Condor bomber unit, K./88, started to re-equip its four squadrons with this type in the summer of 1937, all of them being fully operational by year's end. This aircraft was a machine of 2.K/88.

AIR WAR OVER SPAIN

Above, above right and right: These four Vultee V-1 As were photographed shortly after their arrival at Belleville in France from the USA while in transit to Republican Spain. The snapshots were taken covertly by the Nationalist espionage service.

Above: A view inside the Seville workshops where maintenance of Italian Fiat CR.32s and German Junkers Ju 52s was carried out.

A Fiat CR.32 undergoing overhaul at the workshops in Seville.

THE OUTBREAK OF THE SPANISH CIVIL WAR

Italian pilots enjoy a 'working lunch' in a hangar in Seville.

Nationalist fighter pilots surround capitán Arístides García López, who is wearing Italian flying gear.

In-flight view of an Italian Fiat CR.32. Notice the markings on the upper wing: black bars and white cross.

An Italian escuadrilla of Romeo Ro. 37s, September 1936.

One of the two Caproni Ca 100s sent to Spain by the Italians.

AIR WAR OVER SPAIN

Gourdou Lesseurre GL-32s were used by the Republicans in the North and by their coastal defence unit, Grupo nº 71. Seen here is 'LG-008'. ('Canario' Azaola)

Gourdou Lesseurre GL-32 coded LG-008, Aviación del Norte, 1937
This obsolete French aircraft served in the Aviación del Norte, based at airfields in Santander, Llanes and Carreño, in 1937. Another batch, which arrived in Catalonia in 1938, was part of the Grupo Mixto nº 71 de Defensa de Costas.

engined, Heinkel He 70 *Blitz* of the A.88 reconnaissance unit with its retractable landing gear stood out amongst the general mediocrity of the German equipment.

The Russian personnel and air equipment was concentrated in the *Grupo nº 12*, which was officially established by a *Ministerio de Marina y Aire* order published in the *Diario Oficial* (Gazette), made up of '…volunteer personnel from a single nationality.'

This is the key to the events in the battles of Madrid, the Jarama and especially in Guadalajara, where government aviation, under the excellent command of Russian *general* Jakob Smuschkevich (aka 'Douglas'), experienced the peak period of its existence by far. The *Chato* and *Mosca* fighters excelled with their efficient strafing missions against Italian motorized columns and the Tupolev SB *Katiuskas* tirelessly bombed the enemy rearguard.

The *Legion Condor*

Initially the German airmen constituted a fighter '*Staffel*' equipped with twelve Heinkel He 51s under the command of *Oberleutnant* Eberhardt; a bomber unit with six Junkers Ju 52s known as '*Pedros y Pablos*' commanded by *Oberleutnant* Rudolf von Moreau, and a reconnaissance squadron with six Heinkel He 46s, commanded by *Oberleutnant* Rudolf Loytved-Hardegg. These aircraft operated in the Guadarrama sierra front from Salamanca, Avila, Valladolid, Escalona del Prado, Grajera and Barahona air bases. In October 1936 these airmen operated in the North, in Asturias, and on the Aragon front, recording several claims in the last sector.

In fact, the *Legion Condor* was officially established in November 1936 under the command of *General* Hugo Sperrle, with *Major* Alexander Holle as its Chief of Staff. It was equipped with about 100 aircraft organized as follows:

THE OUTBREAK OF THE SPANISH CIVIL WAR

Early Composition of the *Legion Condor*

Commander: *Gen.* Hugo Sperrle
Chief of Staff: *Maj* Alexander Holle (then *Obstlt.* Wolfram von Richthofen)

Kampfgruppe K/88
(Bomber Group: Junkers Ju 52)
CO: *Maj.* Robert Fuchs
    1. *Staffel*: *Hptm.* Heinz Liegnitz (then *Oblt.* Karl von Knauer)
    2. *Staffel*: *Oblt.* Anselm Brasser (then *Oblt.* Hans-Henning von Beust)
    3. *Staffel*: *Hptm.* Krafft von Delmensingen

Jagdgruppe J/88
(Fighter Group: Heinkel He 51)
CO: *Maj.* Hubertus Merhardt von Bernegg
    1. *Staffel*: *Hptm.* Werner Palm
    2. *Staffel*: *Oblt.* Otto Lehmann
    3. *Staffel*: *Oblt.* Jürgen Roth
    4. *Staffel*: *Oblt.* Kraft Eberhardt

Aufklärungsgruppe A/88
(Strategic Reconnaissance Squadron: Heinkel He 70)
CO: *Hptm.* Heinz Heinsius

Aufklärungsgruppe A/88
(Tactical Reconnaissance Flight: Heinkel He 46)
CO: *Oblt.* Rudolf Loytved-Hardegg

Aufklärungsgruppe See AS/88
(Maritime Reconnaissance Squadron: Heinkel He 59 and He 60)
CO: *Oblt.* Karl-Heinz Wolf (then *Hptm* Erich Kluender)

Flakabteilung F/88
(Anti-Aircraft Section)
CO: *Oberstlt.* Hermann Lichtenberger

Auxiliary units – including:
Sonderstab S/88 (Staff and Staff Flight)
Nachrichtungabteilung LN/88 (Signals)
Park und Luftfahrzeuggruppe P/88 (Salvage and Technical Detachment)

Nationalist Nieuport 52 coded 1-66 in Seville.

A three-aircraft patrol of Nieuport 52 fighters conducts an aerobatic formation manoeuvre over the safety of Republican territory.

39

AIR WAR OVER SPAIN

A Nationalist Fokker F-XII trimotor in the workshops at Leon air base. This aircraft was attacked and set on fire in error by German He 51 fighters in October 1936.

Above and far right: Fiat CR.32s receive maintenance in the open air from an Italian mechanic.

Right: Two government pilots pose for a snapshot on the tail of Dewoitine D.371 '13' of Grupo nº 71 based at Figueras.

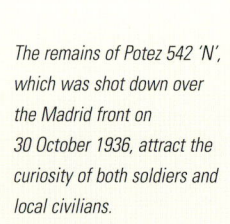

The remains of Potez 542 'N', which was shot down over the Madrid front on 30 October 1936, attract the curiosity of both soldiers and local civilians.

THE OUTBREAK OF THE SPANISH CIVIL WAR

The camouflaged Dewoitine D.372 '9' which carries the red fuselage band of the government forces.

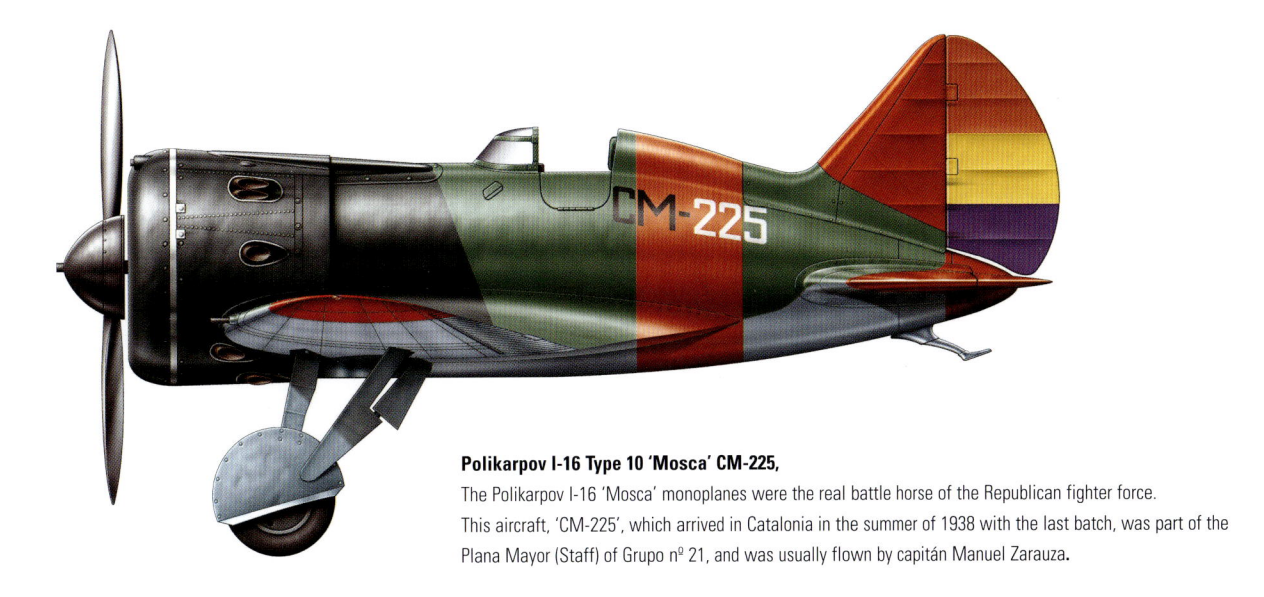

Polikarpov I-16 Type 10 'Mosca' CM-225,
The Polikarpov I-16 'Mosca' monoplanes were the real battle horse of the Republican fighter force.
This aircraft, 'CM-225', which arrived in Catalonia in the summer of 1938 with the last batch, was part of the Plana Mayor (Staff) of Grupo nº 21, and was usually flown by capitán Manuel Zarauza.

Three views of the government's Tupolev SB Katiuska bomber 'White 1' minus its propellers.

41

AIR WAR OVER SPAIN

Polikarpov I-15 Chato coded 'CA-016' was one of the first such Spanish licence-built aircraft; this machine served with Grupo n° 26.

Polikarpov I-15 'Chato' coded CA-193, 2ª Escuadrilla, Grupo nº 26
The agile Polikarpov I-15 'Chato' biplanes equipped the four escuadrillas of Grupo nº 26. This aircraft formed part of the 2ª Escuadrilla.

THE OUTBREAK OF THE SPANISH CIVIL WAR

With parachute strapped to his back, a government pilot in a full leather flying suit climbs into the cockpit of his Chato coded 'CA-131'. ('Canario' Azaola)

A member of the ground crew assists the pilot of a Polikarpov I-15 as he prepares to take off for another mission. Note the long, tubular gun sight fitted through the windshield.

AIR WAR OVER SPAIN

The Polikarpov I-16 Mosca was one of the best aircraft of Soviet origin, being a revolutionary design and the world's first cantilever-winged monoplane fighter with retractable landing gear.

Republican ground crew at work on an evidently well-used Polikarpov I-16 Mosca at a base in northern Spain.

The crew of a Tupolev SB Katiuska: from left to right, Luis Morales (observer), José Miñana (pilot) and Victoriano Sánchez Catalán (air gunner).

44

THE OUTBREAK OF THE SPANISH CIVIL WAR

Sargento José Cobarro López in the observer's position in a Tupolev SB Katiuska bomber with the aircraft's pair of 7.62 mm ShKAS machine guns as its forward armament.

Airmen of the government's Katiuska-equipped Grupo nº 12. Left to right: alférez observador Vicente Ruiz Mateos, teniente piloto José Arcega Nájera (later commander of Grupos nº 12 and nº 24), unidentified alférez mecánico and sargento ametrallador-bombardero Joaquín Pedrerol Borrul.

AIR WAR OVER SPAIN

An in-flight view of a pair of Tupolev SB Katiuskas with aircraft '37' nearest the camera.

Tupolev SB 'Katiuska' coded BK-071 / white '51', 4ª Escuadrilla, Grupo nº 24
The modern Soviet twin-engined Tupolev SB formed the backbone of the Republican bomber force. Ninety-three SBs arrived in Spain, in three batches of 31 each, and served in Grupos nº 12 and nº 24. White '51' was part of the latter's 4ª Escuadrilla.

The burnt-out remains of a Breguet XIX, shot down at Quismondo in October 1936, are examined by soldiers.

Potez 542 coded 'O' was shot down over Teruel in December 1936 with a Spanish crew. (Calparsoro)

THE OUTBREAK OF THE SPANISH CIVIL WAR

Junkers Ju 52s, coded 22-75 and 22-99 – converted 'bombers' of the Legion Condor's K/88 undergo maintenance in the workshop hangar at Seville.

A Heinkel He 111 of the Legion Condor's K/88 undergoes an engine overhaul.

A Dornier Do 17 E-1 reconnaissance aircraft, '27-8', of either the experimental bomber unit, VB/88 or the Aufklärungsgruppe 88 of the Legion Condor. Although intended for reconnaissance, these aircraft often undertook bombing sorties as well.

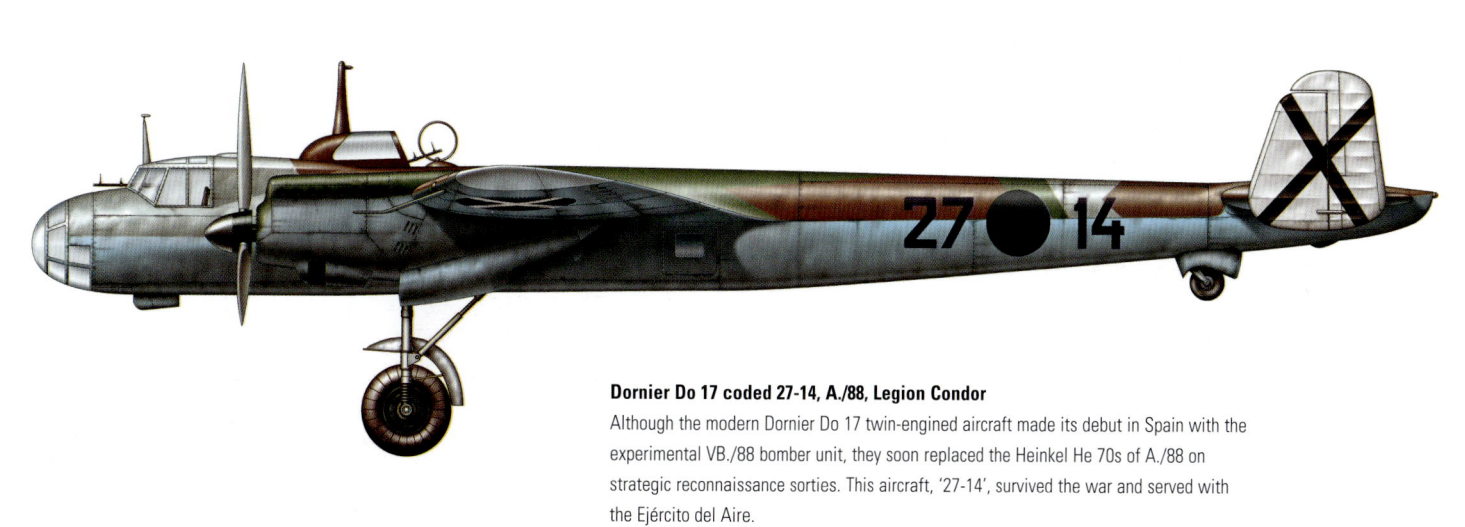

Dornier Do 17 coded 27-14, A./88, Legion Condor
Although the modern Dornier Do 17 twin-engined aircraft made its debut in Spain with the experimental VB./88 bomber unit, they soon replaced the Heinkel He 70s of A./88 on strategic reconnaissance sorties. This aircraft, '27-14', survived the war and served with the Ejército del Aire.

AIR WAR OVER SPAIN

Because the He 60 seaplane was slow and vulnerable to attack, its operations were usually confined to night raids for which the crews developed their own set of tactics. During such operations, the aircraft would effectively glide into the target area with their engines idling, thereby producing as little noise as possible. Over the target, with the bomb load released, the engines were brought back to full power and the crews would hasten their egress from the target area before the defenders had the chance to mount any form of reasonable defence. Eventually however, most Heinkel He 60s were flown by Spanish crews. (E. Herrerra)

Primarily, the 1936 deployment of the cumbersome twin-engined Heinkel He 59 seaplane to Spain was to evaluate air-dropped torpedoes. Later these aircraft scored many successes against Republican shipping including, in January 1937, the capture at sea of the 4,600-ton Republican steamer, Nuria, loaded with Republican troops, merely by tactics of deception and the threat of an aerial torpedo. (E. Herrerra)

THE OUTBREAK OF THE SPANISH CIVIL WAR

A rarely-seen Heinkel He 59 of Aufklärungsgruppe See 88 fitted with Horten torpedoes and carrying the unit's early Totenkopf emblem.

The nose of this Legion Condor Heinkel He 59 floatplane of Aufklärungsgruppe See 88 (AS/88) carries the distinctive Pik As emblem.

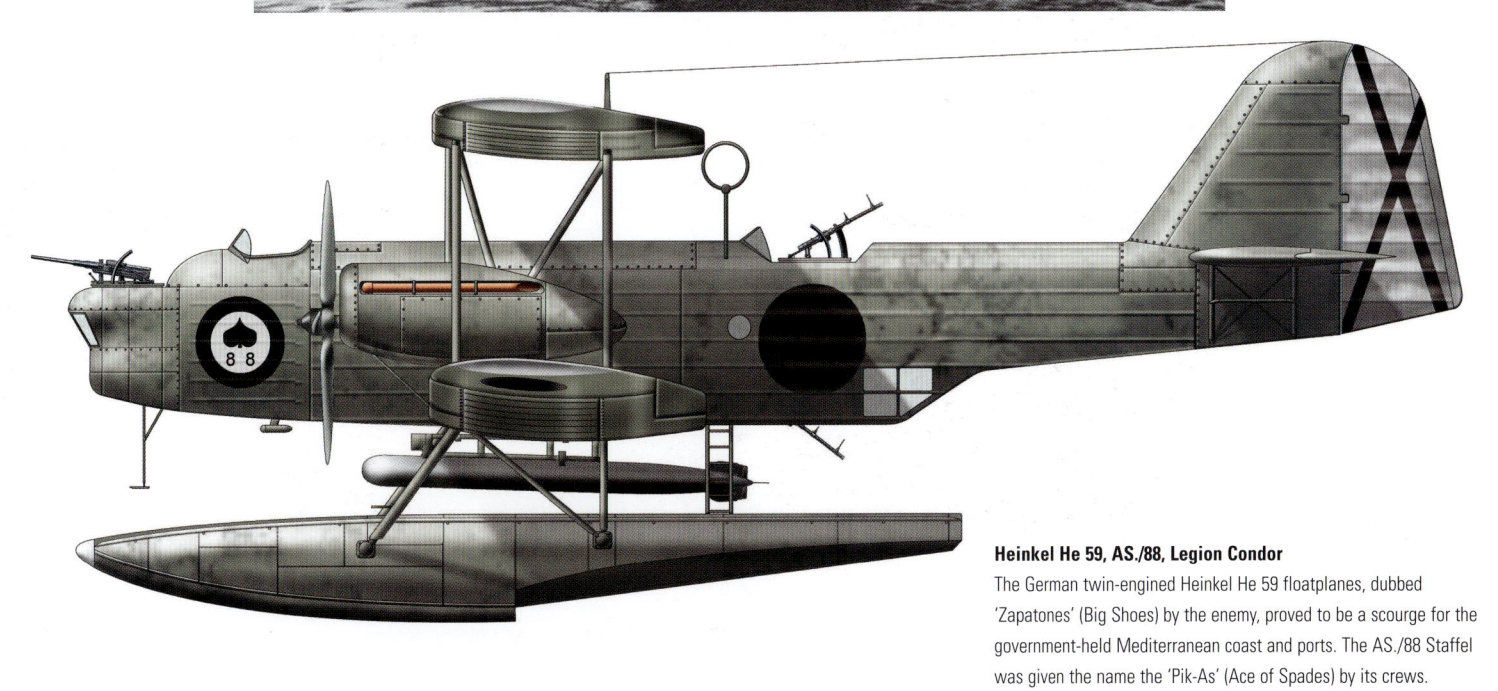

Heinkel He 59, AS./88, Legion Condor
The German twin-engined Heinkel He 59 floatplanes, dubbed 'Zapatones' (Big Shoes) by the enemy, proved to be a scourge for the government-held Mediterranean coast and ports. The AS./88 Staffel was given the name the 'Pik-As' (Ace of Spades) by its crews.

AIR WAR OVER SPAIN

A Junkers Ju 52 W floatplane, coded '527', and used by Aufklärungsgruppe See 88 as a transport. The aircraft carries the skull and crossbones 'Totenkopf' emblem.

Heinkel He 51s were among the first German aircraft to arrive in Spain, in August 1936. Here is aircraft '2-23' of J/88 which carries the 'Zylinderhut' emblem of the unit, seen possibly at Avila in late 1936. (Campesino, via Raúl Arias)

In October 1936 the Republican government bought four Fokker trimotors in France including the one-off F-XX, which was assigned the temporary registration EC-45E. (Salgado)

CHAPTER THREE

THE WAR IN THE AIR: 1937

The battle for Madrid

By early November 1936, during operations directed at the capture of Madrid, the Italian *Aviación Legionaria* formed the bulk of the Nationalist air forces operating on the Madrid Front. Quartered at its main base at Talavera de la Reina, the legion command encountered the nasty surprise of the arrival of new Russian materiel, which considerably reinforced the government's aviation capability.

The new Soviet Polikarpov I-15 and I-16 fighters, as well as the fast twin-engined Tupolev SB *Katiuskas*, were very modern aircraft for the time and proved to be tough opponents in the skies over Madrid. On 5 November a formation of I-15 *Chatos* caught a formation of Fiat CR.32s by surprise and managed to shoot down the commander, *capitano* Maccagno, who was wounded and taken prisoner; he had his right leg amputated. Junkers Ju 52 and Romeo Ro 37 aircraft flown by Spanish crews were also hit and suffered casualties.

Bonomi, in the light of the situation, considered that tactics needed a change and ordered the fighter pilots to take precautionary measures. As he wrote: 'I am issuing orders so that fighter formations over the front shall never be made up of less than fifteen aircraft, their only task being to protect our bombers and to stop the enemy from attacking our lines, and I absolutely prohibit pursuing the enemy by flying into red territory.'

On 13 November, the commanding officer of the second legionnaire Fiat CR.32 squadron, *capitano* Goliardo Mosca, was shot down and killed over the Madrid Front. During this time, the superiority of the Republican Polikarpov I-15 and I-16 fighters continued, a factor which the legionnaire command intended to neutralize with the new aircraft that arrived in Cadiz and Seville later that year. For this reason they had decided to stay on the defensive on the Madrid Front, carrying out only the sorties they considered essential to support the bombers.

By late November, the Italian government had a sufficiently clear view of the situation to ensure the success of the Nationalist cause and what it had to do about it. This required a crucial increase of its support to Franco to tip the balance in his favour once and for all. Mussolini was eager to lend the Nationalists the help they needed, but he wanted guarantees for the future and so the hard negotiations to achieve an Italo-Spanish treaty commenced. On 28 November 1936, Filippo Anfuso, personal secretary to Italy's newly appointed Foreign Minister, Count Ciano, managed to get the secret treaty with the Spanish Nationalists signed.

By late November/early December 1936, the Savoia SM.81s suffered heavy blows as their bases at Gamonal and Velada near Talavera de la Reina (Toledo) were attacked by twin-engined Tupolev SB *Katiuskas* and Polikarpov R.5 *Rasantes*. In the first attack, on 25 November, the enemy bombers destroyed two Romeo Ro.37s and hit a Savoia SM.81. In the following strafing attack, on 4 December, the *Rasantes* seriously damaged three Savoia SM.81s, which had to be sent to Seville for repairs in the Tablada workshops.

Wearing his flying gear, Teniente Manuel Aguirre sits on a car bumper using a typewriter. In the background is Polikarpov I-15 'White 19'.

The secondary fronts

Although there were no organized air units under government control in the north of Spain 'zone', Breguet XIXs, Nieuport 52s, Fokker F.VIIs and militarized civil aircraft were soon sent from Madrid and Catalonia and also

AIR WAR OVER SPAIN

THE WAR IN THE AIR: 1937

Romeo Ro 37 light bombers were used both by Italian and Spanish units. The photograph shows escuadrilla commander, capitán José Muñoz, known as 'El Corto'. ('Canario' Azaola)

AIR WAR OVER SPAIN

For Spanish aviators, standing by an aircraft to embrace a propeller was often seen as a bad omen. However, Teniente Francisco Viñals, commander of the I-15 'Chato'-equipped 2ª Escuadrilla, was apparently not superstitious, for he was downed three times but always escaped unscathed. (J. Salas)

from France, to operate from the air bases at Lasarte at San Sebastián, Lamiaco at Bilbao, La Albericia at Santander and Carreño at Gijón. This *Zona Aérea del Norte* was commanded initially by *capitán* Manuel Cascón, the former commanding officer of *Grupo de caza nº 11* at Getafe. These aircraft were opposed by the *Fuerzas Aéreas* of the Asturias and Santander front, with a Breguet XIX group, a Heinkel He 46 group and a Fokker F.XII group at the León and Burgos air bases. The air bases in Vitoria, Logroño and Saragossa housed another Breguet XIX group, a Heinkel He 46 reconnaissance group, and a Heinkel He 51 fighter squadron to operate both in Biscay and Aragon.

In Andalusia, on the Southern Front, the rebels had the air bases of Seville, Mérida, Córdoba, Antequera and Granada, with a Savoia SM.81 group, a Fiat CR.32 squadron, a Nieuport 52 squadron, and two Breguet XIX groups. As for the government, the Vickers Vildebeests, Breguet XIXs and Nieuport 52s and the Savoia S-62 and Dornier *Wal* seaplanes operated from Los Alcázares, San Javier, Guadix, El Rompedizo and Almería.

In the Balearic Islands, on Majorca, a Savoia SM.81 group and one mixed group with Fiat CR.32 fighters and Macchi M.41 seaplanes were established. On the Republican island of Minorca, there were Savoia S-62 and Dornier *Wal* seaplanes, although they soon retreated to the port of Barcelona.

In Catalonia-Aragon, the Republican air forces made the Sariñena airfield their main base, from where the mixed *Escuadrilla 'Alas Rojas'* ('Red Wings Squadron'), equipped with Breguet XIXs, Vickers Vildebeests, Nieuport 52s, Fokker F.VIIs and De Havilland DH-89 Dragon Rapides operated. In the capital of Aragon, Saragossa, as we have seen, there were Heinkel He 46s and He 51s opposing these aircraft.

January 1937 saw the establishment of the *Zona Aérea Autónoma de Levante*, which would later become the *4ª Región Aérea*, in Valencia from where the bitterly contested Teruel Front was dealt with by late 1936. Breguet XIXs, Potez 540s and Nieuport 52s and Dornier *Wal* and Savoia S.62 seaplanes operated from the Levante air bases.

From 12 March 1937 onwards, the Republican *Subsecretaría del Aire* had two combat arms: the *Fuerzas Aéreas* and the *Defensa Especial Contra Aeronaves* (D.E.C.A. – Special Anti-aircraft Defence).

The expansion of the Italian *Aviación Legionaria*

From the time the *Aviación Legionaria* was established through until late 1936, the *Aviación del Tercio* fighters were organized into three *escuadrillas*: the *1ª Escuadrilla*, which was not active, and the *2ª* and *3ª Escuadrillas* which were based at the Torrijos airfield and combat-ready.

On 28 December 1936, *tenente colonnello* Bonomi was promoted colonel of the Italian *Regia Aeronautica* – although he already enjoyed that rank in Spain – and the new chief commander of the *Aviación Legionaria*, *generale* Velardi, completely reorganized the forces by late 1936 with newly arrived aircraft and their crews.

A new *Grupo de Bombardeo Pesado* (Heavy Bomber Group), equipped with twelve Savoia Marchetti SM.81 trimotors, was organized into two *escuadrillas*, numbers *11ª* and *13ª*, and went operational immediately. The new Savoia SM.81s, along with the few surviving aircraft of the initial group, were used to set up *Grupo de Bombardeo Pesado 'Marelli'* commanded by *tenente colonnello* Ferdinando Rafaelli.

THE WAR IN THE AIR: 1937

An unusual view of the camouflaged wing upper surfaces of Fiat CR. 32s coded 3-20 and 3-22.

A Savoia SM.81 at Tablada, Seville.

A Savoia SM.81 trimotor of the Aviación del Tercio runs up its engines before taxying out at Talavera air base.

AIR WAR OVER SPAIN

A Tupolev SB Katiuska shot down at Motril, Granada on 10 February 1937.

A group of government pilots photographed on 1 May 1937 at La Albericia air base, Santander. Left to right, Zambudio, Rodríguez Panadero, Pedro Lambás, Sánchez de las Matas, González Feo, and three unidentified airmen.

A new Fiat CR.32 fighter squadron had also arrived by late 1936. In January 1937, the Fiat CR.32-equipped *4ª* and *5ª Escuadrillas* were ready for operations while the *6ª Escuadrilla* was established in February 1937.

The *Aviación Legionaria* was completely reorganized in the spring of 1937 and the six Fiat CR.32 fighter squadrons became the *XVI Grupo 'La Cucaracha'* ('The Cockroach') and the *XXIII Grupo 'Asso di Bastoni'* ('Ace of Clubs'). Subsequently, by mid-1937, a third unit was formed, *VIº Grupo 'Leonello'*, also known as '*Gamba di Ferro*' ('Iron Leg'). The name stuck and eventually became official in the spring of 1938 so as to honour the commander, *maggiore* Ernesto Botto, who had lost one leg in combat over the Aragon front in October 1937.

The war in the North

With the battles on the Madrid Front fought to a stalemate, both sides were convinced of the need to abandon direct confrontation, a doctrine so cherished by the followers of Clausewitz. Both General Staffs tried to move the centre of gravity of the war to a secondary Spanish geographical 'zone' that was viewed as more strategically favourable. The government side chose the Extremadura countryside and the Nationalist side chose the Basque territory, which for geographic, orographic, climatic and political reasons, allowed the Nationalist aviation to achieve wide local air superiority, despite its numerical inferiority in the peninsular territory as a whole.

The aviation arm, nominally commanded by *general* Kindelán, placed its bombers at the air bases at Soria and Burgos from where they could reach both the north and central fronts. The lighter aircraft assigned to this sector were deployed to Vitoria.

The Biscay offensive started on 31 March and on 25 April the vanguards of the *Brigadas Navarras* arrived at the foot of mount Oiz, at an equal distance from the towns of Durango and Guernica. *Oberstleutnant* von Richthofen, the Chief of Staff of the *Legion Condor*, asked for the advance to be made on the latter, but *general* Emilio Mola, chief of the *Ejército del Norte*, insisted that Durango was to be occupied first. These differences rendered the famous Guernica air raid, which was carried out on 26 April by Italian and German aircraft, useless, although it resulted only in serious political consequences and propaganda for the Basque cause in particular, and the government forces in general.

The expected Republican offensive on Extremadura did not materialize, because of the fall of the Socialist Francisco Largo Caballero's government and its replacement with that of Juan Negrín,

THE WAR IN THE AIR: 1937

Savoia SM.81 trimotors operated from both Majorca and the peninsula. This aircraft was one of the first to arrive in the Balearic Islands. ('Canario' Azaola)

another Socialist, who was closer to the Communists' military theses. The new government established the *Ministerio de Defensa Nacional*, with four *subsecretarías*: *Ejército*, *Marina*, *Aviación* and *Armamento*, whose direction was assumed by Indalecio Prieto, the former *Ministro de Marina y Aire*.

With the towns of Durango and Guernica now lost, the autonomous authorities of Bilbao tried to push resistance to the limit in the so-called *Cinturón de Hierro* ('Iron Belt'), a concrete defensive line that the local press proclaimed impregnable.

The Nationalist Army timed the assault for 11 June. That day, the German and Italian bombers based at Burgos and Soria were heavily committed in their mission of providing support to the attacking forces. All air units (except for two of the three Junkers Ju 52 squadrons, which could not take off for the second wave) carried out three sorties: the first at 0900 hrs, the second at 1200 hrs and the last at 1900 hrs.

The Nationalist aviation carried out 106 sorties by multi-engined aircraft and 72 by single-engined aircraft on 11 June. The total bomb load dropped exceeded 100 tons.

On 12 June, the *Cinturón de Hierro* line was breached, which facilitated the capture of Bilbao seven days later.

Air supply

Supplying a besieged position was not a new problem to the *Aviación Militar*, as it had already been put into practice in the 1920s during the Morocco campaigns in order to supply blockhouses besieged by Moroccan forces.

However, the case of the medieval Nuestra Señora de la Cabeza religious sanctuary, in the rugged sierra of the province of Jaén in southern Spain, required different methods. The reception area for supplies was much larger than in the case of the African forts; long flights over enemy territory, and continuity, were necessary. There was not a case any longer for 'heroic' lone flights, but rather for regular periodic supply, which had to be carried out in good or bad weather conditions and quite often opposed by enemy fighters and anti-aircraft artillery.

Feeding the 1,000-plus people who were taking refuge in the premises besieged by the government forces required a minimum supply of about 750 kg food a day which could be carried out by a single Junkers Ju 52 or Savoia SM.81 trimotor in just one flight.

Throughout the 205-day siege of Nuestra Señora de la Cabeza sanctuary from 8 October 1936 to 1 May 1937, 167 sorties were carried out which included 121 supply sorties and 45 bombing and reconnaissance sorties.

Subsequently, in September 1937, it was also necessary to supply the defending forces at Belchite by air.

A study of the Italian pilot, tenente Vittorio Stella.

AIR WAR OVER SPAIN

Military personnel and local civilians run up to welcome a Fiat CR. 32 which has landed on a country road.

A mechanic winds the propeller of a Breguet XIX at Sariñena in Huesca. This particular aircraft was detached from Grupo de Reconocimiento Estratégico nº 31 at the air base at Getafe.

One of the government Breguet XIXs detached at Sariñena sported this revolutionary slogan on the under surface of the upper wing – The People's Aviation.

58

THE WAR IN THE AIR: 1937

A Breguet XIX of the Escuadrilla 'Alas Rojas' at Sariñena air base. Note the unit's name on the car door.

Three Republican airmen in full leather flight gear pose for a photograph. In the cente, capitán piloto Armando Gracia, with his Tupolev SB crewmen, capitán observador Juan Caldevilla (right) and teniente bombardero Manuel Gómez (left).

AIR WAR OVER SPAIN

Reconnaissance Heinkel He 70s were handed over to the Spanish upon arrival of more modern Dornier Do 17s and were used to equip Grupo 7G-14 and two independent squadrons. Seen here is a formation of six He 70s of Grupo 7G-14.

This Fiat CR.32, coded 3-6, of the Italian 4ª Escuadrilla legionaria was captured on 29 January 1937. It is seen here at Los Alcázares air base.

60

THE WAR IN THE AIR: 1937

Finally, almost at the end of the civil war, in missions of pure propaganda, the Nationalist bombers dropped bread on the government cities of Madrid and Barcelona, in an attempt to demoralize the hungry population of the Republic.

The battle of Brunete

Since March 1937, during the Biscay campaign, the three *Gruppen* of the *Legion Condor* equipped with aircraft with retractable landing gear had proved their high quality in terms of build and performance. One of these *Gruppen* was a mixed experimental bombing unit, *Versuchsbombenstaffel* VB/88, equipped with Heinkel He 111, Dornier Do 17 and Junkers Ju 86 twin-engined fast bombers. The second, the reconnaissance unit, *Aufklärungsgruppe* A/88, was equipped with Heinkel He 70 *Blitz* single-engined reconnaissance aircraft, and the third, 2.J/88, had Messerschmitt Bf 109 B monoplane fighters. In the North however, the Messerschmitts were confronted only by Polikarpov I-15 *Chatos*, which managed to shoot down just one of the first Dornier Do 17s in combat.

This superiority of the modern German aircraft had to contend with the Russian Polikarpov I-16 *Mosca* monoplanes. The three German units had been supplemented by another unit of Italian Savoia SM.79 trimotors in April 1937, which had also made their debut on the Northern Front.

The real confrontation took place during the battle of Brunete in July 1937, when the *Ejército Popular* enjoyed overwhelming air superiority during the first few days thanks to its Polikarpov

Fiat CR.32s of the 3ª Escuadrilla of the Aviación legionaria.

The Italian capitano Dequal, with moustache, seen centre, with pilots of his CR.32-equipped escuadrilla, 'La Cucaracha'.

AIR WAR OVER SPAIN

Republican fighter pilots in the North. Left to right: Zambudio, Rodríguez Panadero, González Feo, Baquedano and Sánchez de las Matas.

Polikarpov I-16 Mosca 'White 154' photographed in a dismantled state by mechanics at an air base in the North while awaiting to be taken away for overhaul.

Maintenance work on a Soviet-made Polikarpov I-16 at a forward airfield during the northern campaign.

I-16 *Mosca* and I-15 *Chato* fighter squadrons and its two *Grupos* of twin-engined Tupolev SB *Katiuskas*, nº *12* and nº *24*, which outnumbered and outclassed their Italo-German equivalent, but which were inferior in bomb load capacity. It also had a *Grupo de Bombardeo Ligero nº 30* (Light Bomber Group 30), and three *escuadrillas independientes*, nº *20*, nº *40* and nº *50*, all of them equipped with Polikarpov R.Z *Natacha* aircraft.

The Messerschmitt Bf 109 Bs, which were at a clear numerical disadvantage against the Polikarpov I-16s, proved that they could be excellent fighter aircraft as soon as their greatest handicap – lack of power – was ironed out. The numerical superiority of the Fiat CR.32 over the Polikarpov I-15 *Chato* partly compensated for this inferiority in Nationalist monoplane fighters.

The Republican aviation introduced a great tactical innovation in this battle: the creation of a night fighter flight, equipped with Polikarpov I-15 *Chatos*, which in the last days of the operations over Brunete claimed two Junkers Ju 52s of the *Legion Condor*, which were credited to Russian pilots, Mikhail Yakushin and Anatoli Serov.

The battle of Brunete ended in a stalemate and something similar was to happen later at Belchite, Saragossa.

THE WAR IN THE AIR: 1937

A broken-down Koolhoven FK.51 recovered by truck on the North front where such aircraft were used as light bombers.

The end of the war in the north of Spain
After the fall of Bilbao, with that town in rebel hands and the ensuing capture of the whole province of Biscay, by early July 1937 the *Ejército Popular de la República* deployed the Polikarpov I-16 *Mosca* fighters of *4ª Escuadrilla* together with all its Russian pilots, to Santander and on the same date, the Polikarpov I-15 *Chatos* of the *Escuadrilla de Caza del Norte* were also reinforced with one more Spanish expeditionary unit, commanded by *capitán* Ramón Puparelli Francia.

On 17 August the Polikarpov I-16 *Mosca* fighters of *3ª Escuadrilla*, with Spanish pilots trained in the Soviet Union and Russian flight leaders, arrived at La Albericia, Santander, by which time the offensive on the province had already started. These four government fighter units did not manage to stop the seven squadrons of the opposing Nationalist aviation, six Italian Fiat CR.32 squadrons and one German *Staffel* of Messerschmitt Bf 109s, although the Republican pilots fought very courageously.

On 1 October the *Escuadra de Caza* and the *Chato*-equipped *Grupo nº 26* were placed under Spanish command, which was already the case with the *Escuadra de Bombardeo* and its *Grupos nº 24* and *nº 30*.

By mid-October the *Ejército Popular* launched a new offensive on Saragossa, unsuccessful on land but very successful in the air – especially the strafing of General Sanjurjo's air base in Saragossa on the 15th by 21 Polikarpov I-15 *Chato* biplanes of the *1ª* and *2ª Escuadrillas* of *Grupo nº 26*, escorted by 43 Polikarpov I-16 *Mosca* monoplanes of the *Grupo nº 21* (five squadrons and all but *4ª Escuadrilla*, which was deployed to the North). In this surprise attack, 12 aircraft were destroyed on the ground and 16 damaged, five of them seriously.

In Asturias, Kindelán's aviation, now with two Heinkel He 111 and two Messerschmitt Bf 109 squadrons, saw intense and efficient operations that culminated with the sinking of a destroyer and a submarine in the port of Gijón, shortly before the end of the strong Asturian resistance on 21 October.

Out of over 200 aircraft operating from the air bases on the Biscay coast, only seven managed to escape to France: two Polikarpov I-15 *Chato* biplanes, a Polikarpov I-16 *Mosca* and four more aircraft. Thus, about 200 aircraft, 40 per cent of the Polikarpov I-15 and I-16 fighters imported from Russia, were lost on the Biscay coast. However, Polikarpov I-16 *Mosca* losses were easily replaced thanks to the arrival of 62 fighters of the type in August, which were used to establish the *6ª Escuadrilla* of *Grupo nº 21*, while the *3ª* and *4ª Escuadrillas* lost in the North were reformed. Quite a different case was that of the I-15 *Chato* biplanes, of which only *Escuadrillas 1ª* and *2ª* of *Grupo nº 26* remained active, as well as the *3ª Escuadrilla* which was being created at Figueras in Gerona and a fourth *escuadrilla* that was established next; they were opposed by ten Fiat CR.32 fighter *escuadrillas*, although numbers of both these aircraft types, which arrived in Spain up until September, were around 150.

The battle of Teruel
The result of the campaign in the North encouraged the Germans and Italians to reinforce the side they thought was now victorious. Until January 1938, both countries had sent to Spain a total of 106

fighters: 86 Fiat CR.32 biplanes and 20 Messerschmitt Bf 109s, as well as 87 fast multi-engined bombers, as compared to just 49 Polikarpov I-15 *Chato* and 31 Tupolev SB *Katiuska* twin-engined aircraft received by the government aviation, a disproportion that did not cease to increase until the end of the civil war. This flow of materiel allowed Nationalists to establish the *1ª Brigada Aérea Hispana*, to supply the *Legion Condor's* K/88 with 35 Heinkel He 111s and to start the creation of two *escuadras* of Savoia SM.79 trimotors, both in the Peninsula and in the Balearic Islands, with a total of 25 trimotors by late 1937, and a further 18 aircraft of this type flown by Spanish crews.

General Franco wanted to retake direct control on the Madrid Front but he did so in a hesitant manner, which the *Ejército Popular de la República* used to to take the opportunity to mount an offensive in the secondary sector of Teruel on 15 December 1937, the first province capital they managed to capture during the conflict.

On the political front, by late January 1938, Franco's first government had been established, which for the first time ever included a *Ministerio de Defensa* and a *Subsecretaría del Aire* for the Nationalist side.

The numerous Polikarpov I-16 *Mosca* losses in the endless combats during the battle of Teruel forced the headquarters of *Grupo nº 21* to disband its *3ª* and *6ª Escuadrillas*. However, the Polikarpov I-15 *Chato*s managed to keep the four *escuadrillas* of *Grupo nº 26* operational and a night fighter squadron was created thanks to production at the SAF. 3/16 aircraft factory, established in Reus and Sabadell.

As regards the rest of the main aircraft of *coronel* Ignacio Hidalgo de Cisneros' *Aviación*, the 31 Tupolev SB *Katiuska* bombers of the batch that arrived in the winter of 1937 allowed both the creation of the *4ª Escuadrilla* of *Grupo nº 24* and the operations of the *escuadrillas* at full strength.

As far as pilot training was concerned, the Second Course of airmen trained in Russia arrived in Republican Spain simultaneously to the First Course trained in Italy for the Nationalists.

The Messerschmitt Bf 109 B-1 represented technical and tactical innovation. Here Bf 109 '6-12' of Jagdgruppe 88 displays its Zylinder Hut unit emblem. The aircraft suffered a crash-landing at Santander-West whilst flown by Uffz. Hermann Stange. Stange was to shoot down three Republican aircraft in Spain (Campesino via Raúl Arias)

THE WAR IN THE AIR: 1937

Bf 109 D-1, '6-53', the third such variant to be delivered to Spain photographed in the summer of 1938. It was powered by the Junkers Jumo 210 Da twelve-cylinder inverted-Vee liquid cooled in-line engine (C. O'Donnell)

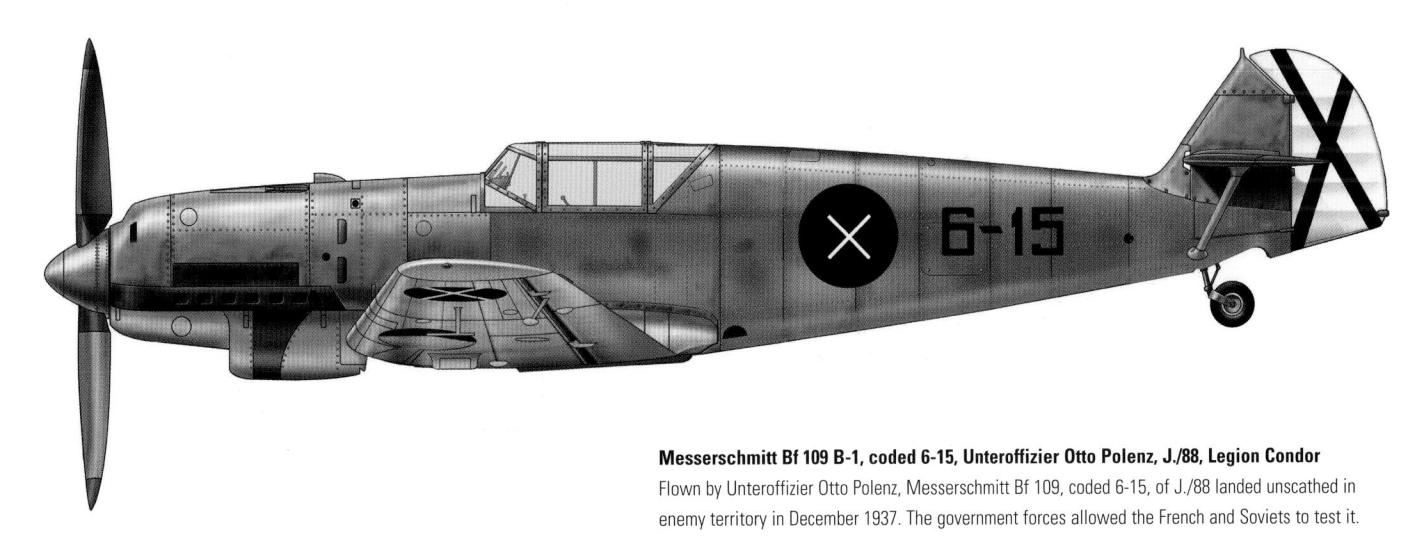

Messerschmitt Bf 109 B-1, coded 6-15, Unteroffizier Otto Polenz, J./88, Legion Condor
Flown by Unteroffizier Otto Polenz, Messerschmitt Bf 109, coded 6-15, of J./88 landed unscathed in enemy territory in December 1937. The government forces allowed the French and Soviets to test it.

AIR WAR OVER SPAIN

An unusual view of a Heinkel He 70 Blitz of the Legion Condor. The aircraft was dubbed Rayo in Spain, the translation of its original German name.

A pair of Heinkel He 70 Blitz of A/88 on patrol over Spanish territory.

THE WAR IN THE AIR: 1937

This Heinkel He 70 of the Legion Condor is seen having made a possible collision with another aircraft on the airfield.

A mechanic at work on the engine of a Mosca sheltered from both the sun and enemy eyes among the trees of a Republican air base during the northern campaign in 1937.

AIR WAR OVER SPAIN

Capitán observador Antonio Blanch Rodríguez of the Grupo nº 12 'Katiuskas'.

Two views of Tupolev SB Katiuska 'White 2'.

THE WAR IN THE AIR: 1937

Two views of a captured Tupolev SB Katiuska in Nationalist markings being 'put through its paces'.

AIR WAR OVER SPAIN

Teniente José Falcó was the last commander of the Republican Escuadrilla de Caza Nocturna.

'Mosca' nº 35 was downed during the battle of Brunete by tenente Tocci's Fiat CR-32s in July 1937.

The Republican Koolhoven FK.51, coded '8', had to make a forced-landing in France in May 1937 while on transit to Bilbao. Here, Gendarmes keep an eye on the aircraft.

THE WAR IN THE AIR: 1937

Teniente piloto Juan Lario with his Polikarpov I-15 while with 2ª Escuadrilla of Grupo nº 26.

Capitán Juan Comas Borrás was successively commander of Polikarpov I-15 'Chato'-equipped 3ª Escuadrilla and then of Grupo nº 26.

The remains of Chato 'CA-34' of 4ª Escuadrilla of Grupo nº 26 loaded onto a truck ready to be transported for salvage – or to be cannibalised for spares. (Campesino, via Raúl Arias)

AIR WAR OVER SPAIN

Clad in leather flying gear and equipped with a parachute, a government fighter pilot prepares to board his I-15. Note the fitting of the gunsight.

Republican pilots of 3ª Escuadrilla of Grupo nº 26, commanded by capitán Juan Comas Borrás at La Señera.

Teniente Antonio Nieto Sandoval, commander of the 3ª Escuadrilla, with sargento José Garre Solano at Monjos airfield.

72

THE WAR IN THE AIR: 1937

Six Heinkel He 111s of the Legion Condor's K/88 in line abreast formation somewhere over Spain. (Calparsoro)

A Savoia SM.79 of the Aviación Legionaria based in the Balearic Islands. By late 1937, two escuadras of SM.79 trimotors were operating over the Peninsula and the Balearics. ('Canario' Azaola)

AIR WAR OVER SPAIN

A Savoia SM.79, coded '5', of the Italian Sorci Verdi group photographed after a forced-landing. ('Canario' Azaola)

Pilots of the 3ª Escuadrilla of Grupo nº 24. At centre is capitán Armando Gracia, the unit's commander.

Capitán Armando Gracia, commander of the 3ª Escuadrilla de Katiuskas, Grupo nº 24.

The flying personnel of 3ª Escuadrilla of Grupo nº 24 line up for a photograph in their flight gear with one of their unit's Tupolev SB Katiuska bombers as a backdrop.

CHAPTER FOUR

THE WAR IN THE AIR: 1938

The Nationalist offensive on Aragon and the race to the sea
The breakthrough of the government zone

IN March 1938, for the first time ever in the conflict, *general* Kindelán's aviation was deployed on a larger number of air bases in Aragon than the Republican aviation. For the great struggle that was expected, the commanding general of the *Ejército del Norte*, Fidel Dávila, had gathered 21 divisions in Aragon, against which the Republican *general*, Vicente Rojo, could oppose 18, 11 of them on both sides of the Ebro, two as immediate reserves and another five slightly towards the rear.

On 9 March, the *Cuerpo de Ejército Marroquí*, the Italian CTV and the *Cuerpo de Ejército de Galicia* moved off south of the Ebro, supported by García Valiño's *Agrupación* (Task Force), in a great offensive operation that culminated in the arrival at the Mediterranean in the Vinaroz-Benicarló area and the cutting of the Republican zone in two. The *Legion Condor* operated in cooperation with the *Cuerpo de Ejército Marroquí*, the *Aviación Legionaria* with the CTV and the *Brigada Aérea Hispana* and the Spanish independent *grupos* with the *Cuerpo de Ejército de Galicia*.

On the first day of the offensive, the air units broke all their performance records and dropped 210 tons of bombs. The Republican aviation saw its first mass sortie, with a formation of 35 fighters, but this operation was postponed until 1800 hrs, when the lines of two of the three divisions of the *XII Cuerpo de Ejército* had already been broken and the fate of Belchite and Muniesa was sealed.

From 11 March onwards, the government aviation did its utmost, especially the *Escuadra de Caza nº 11*, which was four times over the front on that day, with 155 fighter sorties. Despite this effort, Dávila's troops reached the banks of the Guadalope river on the 17th.

The month of March had seen the annexation of Austria by Hitler's Germany, and France pondered the possibility of taking a direct part in the war in Spain; the *Comité Permanent de la Défense Nationale* held a session in Paris on the 15th in order to discuss this matter. Mussolini, aware of this possibility, ordered his air forces in the Balearic Islands, without the knowledge of Spanish headquarters, to bomb Barcelona sporadically, which started on the night of the 16th and ended at 1500 hrs on the 18th. In total, seventeen attacks were carried out and 44 tons of bombs were dropped, twice as many as over Guernica.

A few days later, 30 disassembled Polikarpov I-16 type 10 *Mosca* fighters crossed the border from the Pyrenees. They were armed with four machine guns and, once assembled, were used to equip the two Russian *escuadrillas*, numbers *2ª* and *5ª*. These two units handed over their I-16 type 6 *Mosca* aircraft to the Spanish *1ª* and *4ª Escuadrillas* and the *3ª Escuadrilla* was reactivated on 10 April, with a Spanish command and Spanish pilots.

The offensive widened on 22 March north of the Ebro, with great success, and the *Cuerpo de Ejército Marroquí*, which crossed the river, advanced on Los Monegros and managed to reach Lérida on 4 April. South of the Ebro, the advance to the sea along the river as intended was not possible, but the *Cuerpo de Ejército de Galicia* made its way to Morella and from there to Vinaroz, Benicarló and the Ebro delta.

Heinkel He 111 '25-43' of K/88 on its landing approach. During April 1938, elements of K/88 were re-equipped with the He 111 J with DB 600 engines, and took part in 'Operation Neptun', a concentrated attack against Republican naval forces in the ports of Cartagena and Almería.

One of the two Dewoitine D-510 fighter monoplanes of the Republican aviation photographed at an unidentified air base in 1938.

AIR WAR OVER SPAIN

Canadian-built Grumman GE 23 Delfines were first deployed with Grupo nº 28 and then with Grupo nº 71.

Sargento Andrés Fierro Ménu landed this Polikarpov I-16 Mosca, coded CM-192, at the Nationalist air base at Almenar, Lérida on 13 September 1938.

Teniente piloto Juan Lario posing by his Grumman GE.23 Delfín 'White 5'.

The offensive on Valencia

The exploitation of success in an unexpected direction brought about, as a result, three months of slow advances by *general* Dávila's troops and one single practical outcome: the capture of Castellón in June, but the taking of Valencia, the expected final goal, was not achieved.

All of the operational government aircraft were concentrated on the air bases of the *4ª Región Aérea*, from where they had to engage the *Legion Condor*, the *Aviación Legionaria* and the Nationalist aviation.

With 34 Grumman GE.23 *Delfín* fighter aircraft that had arrived in Catalonia from Canada via France, the new *Grupo nº 28* was established in May, and it was operational by late June 1938. The Nationalist fighters were reinforced with a third *escuadrilla* of the Messerschmitt Bf 109 C and D types, highly improved over the previous B model.

The battle of the Ebro

On 25 July 1938, the *Ejército Popular de la República*, namely the *Ejército del Ebro*, opened the most important but most technically challenging and militarily difficult offensive action of the whole war, starting it with a level of success it had never before enjoyed.

Throughout August, 90 Polikarpov I-16 type 10s were assembled in Figueras, from a batch shipped to the French Atlantic coast, which allowed the equipping of the six *escuadrillas* of *Grupo nº 21* and even created a *7ª Escuadrilla*.

It was at this stage of the war, that both aeronautical adversaries reached their zenith in terms of operational potential; the serviceable 176 Polikarpov I-16, I-15 and Grumman GE.23 *Delfín* fighters slightly outnumbered the 168 Fiat CR.32 and Messerschmitt Bf 109 (96 Italian and 36 Spanish Fiat CR.32s, and 36 German Bf 109s), which explains the intense air action during this battle. In terms of bombers, there was an abysmal disproportion for the Republicans between the 135 Italo-German fast multi-engined aircraft and the thirty-seven Tupolev SB *Katiuskas*.

Older fixed-landing gear aircraft on both sides could hardly operate in the Ebro area, given the large number of fighters and the high-density and high-quality anti-aircraft guns packed into such a small territory. They remained useful on secondary theatres of operations, however, such as in Extremadura and Andalusia, or in the field of coastal defence.

The Republican *Fuerzas Aéreas*: Aircraft strength during the battle of the Ebro

7 August 1938

Aircraft type	I-16	I-15	SB	*Delfín*	RZ	Misc	Total
Operational	41	51	33	18	39	28	210
Servicing	10	4	4	3	2	11	34
Total	**51**	**55**	**37**	**21**	**41**	**39**	**244**

16 August 1938, Catalonia

Aircraft type	I-16	I-15	SB	*Delfín*	RZ	Misc	Total
Operational	50	36	18	9	11	20	144
Servicing	21	5	1	–	–	6	33
Total	**71**	**41**	**19**	**9**	**11**	**26**	**177**

Central Southern Zone

Aircraft type	I-16	I-15	SB	*Delfín*	RZ	Misc	Total
Operational	–	13	10	11	29	–	63
Servicing	–	2	2	–	2	–	6
Subtotal	–	15	12	11	31	–	69
Total	**71**	**56**	**31**	**20**	**42**	**–**	**220**

6 September 1938

Aircraft type	I-16	I-15	SB	*Delfín*	RZ	Misc	Total
Operational	76	52	22	19	38	25	232
Servicing	19	4	5	–	2	8	38
Total	**95**	**56**	**27**	**19**	**40**	**33**	**234**
Pilots	146	145	44	21	60	202	618

1 October 1938, Catalonia

Aircraft type	I-16	I-15	SB	*Delfín*	RZ	Misc	Total
Operational	52	39	8	9	11	16	135
Servicing	17	–	2	–	–	7	26
Total	**69**	**39**	**10**	**9**	**11**	**23**	**161**

Central Southern Zone

Aircraft type	I-16	I-15	SB	*Delfín*	RZ	Misc	Total
Operational	14	25	16	10	29	6	100
Servicing	1	–	–	–	–	–	1
Subtotal	15	25	16	10	29	6	101
Total	**84**	**64**	**26**	**19**	**40**	**29**	**262**

At the height of the battle, on the Republican side, the last Soviet airmen were repatriated, while on the Nationalist side, the Italians disbanded *Grupo de Caza nº VI 'Gamba di Ferro'* and the Savoia SM.81 *Escuadra nº 21*. The latter was replaced with the Spanish *4ª* and *5ª Escuadras*, with 12 aircraft each. Furthermore, Nationalist aviation expanded with the establishment of the *6ª Escuadra* with some twin-engined Caproni Ca.310 bombers just purchased from Italy. The Republican aviation managed to import high-altitude Wright Cyclone engines to equip the *4ª Escuadrilla* of *Grupo nº 21*.

On 16 November, the *Ejército del Ebro* had to cross the river and pull back to the East, after having managed to postpone the outcome of the war for nearly four months, but without any practical advantage, as the imminent danger of a world war vanished after the Munich Conference.

The fall of Catalonia

This campaign by the Nationalist forces opened on 23 December 1938 in very bad weather in the north of Catalonia. The Italian Fiat CR.32 fighters in the Peninsula numbered 78 at this time, whereas the Spanish equivalent had increased to 62, of which 54 were at front-line air bases and eight receiving overhaul. On the government side, the serviceable Polikarpov I-16 *Moscas* had decreased to 60, in five *escuadrillas* of *Grupo nº 21* (as *2ª* and *5ª Escuadrillas* had been disbanded) and reserves were very low. The Messerschmitt Bf 109s and the Polikarpov I-15 *Chato* had hardly changed in numbers as compared to the four previous months, during the battle of the Ebro, but a few Messerschmitt Bf 109 E with three-blade propellers – very superior to the B, C and D types available so far – had already arrived in Spain.

Government aircraft losses during December 1938 were very numerous; according to *mayor* Andrés García Lacalle, commanding officer of *Escuadra de Caza nº 11*, they were thirty-four. These aircraft losses comprised 12 Polikarpov I-15 *Chatos*, 11 Polikarpov I-16 *Moscas*, two Tupolev SB *Katiuskas* and nine Polikarpov RZ *Natacha* light bombers, of which only the Polikarpov I-15 biplanes could be replenished without difficulty.

Capitán Andrés García Lacalle talks with coronel Núñez Maza, the Air Undersecretary, at a banquet. In the foreground, aviation commissar, Belarmino Tomás.

Andrés García Lacalle (Sestao, Biscay 1909 – Mexico, 1976)

At the start of the military uprising, *sargento piloto* Lacalle was part of the Nieuport 52-equipped *Grupo de Caza nº 11, 2ª Escuadrilla* at Getafe and shot down several aircraft while flying Nieuport 52s, Dewoitine 372s, Loire 46s and Hawker Spanish Furies during the early combats over the Sierra de Madrid. He was then deployed on the Extremadura front. Flying a Fury, he saw great successes over the Talavera de la Reina area, in Toledo, facing Fiat CR.32s and Junkers Ju 52s. He was promoted *alférez* in September. In November, he was posted to Pavel Richagov's Polikarpov I-15-equipped *escuadrilla* and operated uninterrupted over Madrid, first flying as left wingman to Russian flight leader Iván Kopèts, and then as flight leader himself. According to Russian sources, he was credited with one kill during that time. He was promoted *teniente* in November, then *capitán* in January 1937, and mentioned in dispatches. Shortly afterwards, we were given command of the first Spanish I-15-equipped *escuadrilla*, initially known as *Escuadrilla Lacalle*, which included an American-manned flight. The unit arrived at the former Hispano-Suiza factory airfield at Guadalajara on 7 February and made its debut during the battle of the Jarama. It performed well but also experienced losses: José Calderón, Ben Leider and Luis Bercial were killed, while Americans Jim Allison and Harold Dahl were shot down. According to the American pilot, Frank Tinker, at that time Lacalle had been credited with eleven kills. Tinker saw him as a good leader but others, like Tarazona and Sayós, did not share his opinion.

During the battle of Guadalajara things turned easier, although the *Escuadrilla Lacalle* suffered one casualty, *teniente piloto* Antonio Blanch of the *Aeronáutica Naval*, and a prisoner, Guatemalan Manuel García Gómez, who was later exchanged. Once the battle was over, García Lacalle was relieved. In June 1937, he was sent to the Soviet Union as accompanying instructor of the 2nd Pilot Course at Pilot School No. 20 at Kirovabad, sharing command with a Soviet officer. Back in Spain, he was posted to the Pilot Pool at the Celrá air base in Gerona for a short time. After the Barcelona air raids, he was appointed chief of the air and coastal defence of Catalonia. In May 1938, he was committed with the organization of the new assault and coastal defence Grumman GE-23 *Delfín*-equipped *Grupo nº 28*. He led the group in the early operations of the battle of the Ebro. Attached as liaison officer to *general* Rojo's and *coronel* Modesto's Command Post, he did not often fly and later, he operated with his GE-23 unit on the East front at Lérida. In October, he handed over command and on 22 December was appointed deputy commander of the *Escuadra de Caza nº 11* during the battle of Catalonia. On 30 November 1938, García Lacalle had been promoted *mayor* and mentioned in dispatches.

On 6 February 1939 he evacuated the Vilajuiga air base in Gerona fighting his way out and landed his *Chato* at Francazal in Toulouse, France. There he was questioned by *Armeé de l'Air* officers. He moved to Mexico, thence to the Dominican Republic, and eventually back to Mexico, where he settled.

The number of Polikarpov I-16 monoplanes in Catalonia decreased on 8 January 1939 when ten of them, belonging to the *1ª Escuadrilla* of *Grupo nº 21*, flew southwards to take part in the planned government offensive, and was reduced again on 12 January, when four I-16 *Moscas* were destroyed and a further ten also damaged in a strafing raid over Monjos air base. For the government airmen, only a kind of guerrilla-style air war was possible now, in surprise actions, when conditions were favourable, but even on such occasions that they did deploy, successes were elusive.

In January and February 1939, 174 aircraft arrived in Catalonia from the Soviet Union including about 30 more modern Polikarpov I-15 bis *Superchatos* but an additional 144 aircraft were returned because there was no time to assemble them. This was the last batch to be ordered from Moscow by *general* Hidalgo de Cisneros to be delivered, but it did not arrive in time.

Over 100 aircraft arrived in Nationalist Spain from Germany and Italy. These comprised 50 Messerschmitt Bf 109 Es, 39 Heinkel He 111 Es, 11 Heinkel He 112s and ten Fiat G.50 monoplane fighters and other aircraft of lesser importance, which were used to reequip the fighter and bomber units of the *Legion Condor*, J/88 and K/88, and to establish the new mixed (Bf 109 and He 112) *Grupo de Caza 5-G-5* and *Escuadra nº 7* fighter units of the Nationalist aviation, as well as an Italian *Grupo Experimental*.

THE WAR IN THE AIR: 1938

One of the first Moscas to be captured was repaired and flown by the Nationalists and coded '1W-1'. (F. Ezquerro)

In the later stages of the civil war, Heinkel He 51 fighters had to be relegated to the cadena – strafing – role. Seen here are He 51 B-1s '2-102' and '2-115', among the last to be handed over to the Spanish by the Legion Condor. The latter aircraft was flown by Dr. Heinrich Neumann, one of the Legion Condor medical officers. An amateur pilot, Neumann often used to fly to the various airfields where his patients were based, but this practice came to an end when he crashed an He 51 on 5 December 1937. The machine shown here had a red cross thinly outlined in white superimposed over its black national insignia disc. The legend painted on the side of the fuselage read: 'Tut mir nichts, ich tu Euch auch nichts!' ('If you don't bother me, I won't bother you!'). (Campesino, via Raúl Arias)

Ten Fiat G.50 fighters arrived in Spain from Italy almost at the end of the war and equipped the Nationalist Grupo Experimental de Caza. ('Canario' Azaola)

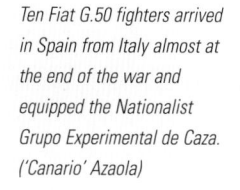

Heinkel He 112 were purchased by the Nationalist aviation and immediately equipped the Spanish Grupo 5-G-5. Two such machines, '5-51' and '5-52', are seen here shortly after delivery. ('Canario' Azaola)

79

CHAPTER FIVE
1939: THE END OF THE SPANISH CIVIL WAR

Pozoblanco-Peñarroya: the last government offensive

In order to postpone, as much as possible, the very likely attack on Catalonia, the government headquarters planned an operation in the Pozoblanco-Peñarroya sector, as well as a landing in the Motril zone. The latter had to be abandoned and only the ground campaign was set about, in which the Republican aviation sent the three *escuadrillas* of Polikarpov *Natachas* of *Grupo nº 30*, two *escuadrillas* of Tupolev SB *Katiuskas* of *Grupo nº 24* and two Polikarpov I-15 *Chato* and one Polikarpov I-16 *Mosca* fighter *escuadrilla*. They were countered by a Fiat CR.32 *Grupo de Caza*, the Junkers Ju 52 and Savoia SM.81 bomber *escuadras* and Heinkel He 51, Aero A 101 and Heinkel He 45 cooperation aircraft.

During the operation, with initial success for the government, several combats took place. In one of these combats, *capitán* Vázquez Sagastizábal, commander of one of the Nationalist Fiat CR.32 *escuadrillas*, was killed and was awarded a posthumous *Cruz Laureada de San Fernando*.

Joaquín García Morato Castaño (Melilla, 1904 – Griñón, 1939)

One of the most accomplished pilots of the *Aviación Militar*, Morato trained as a pilot in 1925 and qualified on fighter, seaplane and multi-engine types, as well as in instrument and aerobatic flying. In 1930 he was appointed an instructor and promoted *capitán* in 1935. At the start of the military uprising, Morato was abroad, but reported to the rebel authorities. He was soon flying Nieuports in Seville and Cordoba and scored his first successes on Vickers Vildebeests, Breguets and Nieuports over the Andalusia front. He flew Heinkel He 51s when they arrived and scored several successes on the Extremadura and Andalusia sectors, including some Potez 540s. But it was with the arrival of the CR.32 that García Morato found his real 'war horse', scoring most of his 40 kills flying '3-51'. During the battle of the Jarama, leading the so-called 'Patrulla Azul' made up of *tenientes* Bermúdez de Castro and Salvador and himself, he scored his greatest success when confronting the fast and manoeuvrable Soviet Polikarpov I-15s and I-16s. The combat of 18 February 1937 brought him the *Cruz Laureada de San Fernando*; his wingmen received the *Medalla Militar colectiva*.

Acting *comandante* Morato officially remained a *capitán* throughout the whole war. He led the first Spanish CR.32 *Grupo, 2G-3*, during the battles of La Granja, Zaragoza, Brunete and Santander and was eventually posted to the headquarters of the *1ª Brigada del Aire*. He flew all new fighter types, including Bf 109s and Heinkel He 112s and assumed command of a new *Grupo 3G-3* and later the *7ª Escuadra de Caza*, a mixed CR.32/Bf 109-equipped unit.

In June 1938, he distinguished himself again when confronting, alone, a large formation of RZ Natachas, for which he was proposed for a posthumous second *Cruz Laureada*, which was not awarded. Four days after the end of the war, on 4 April, García Morato died in an accident at the Griñón air base, while taking part in the making of a German propaganda film.

Coronel Casado's *coup d'état* and disaster in Cartagena

On 27 February 1939, the governments of Britain and France recognized *general* Franco's government, as a result of which, the President of the Spanish Republic, Manuel Azaña, then in France, resigned. This event was also used by the Republican Chief-of-Staff, *general* Vicente Rojo, to stay in France too, not to return to Spain until the 1960s.

On the previous day, the president of the government and Defence Minister, the Socialist Juan Negrín, had decided to continue the war, even against the opinion of most of the government's senior military commanders during a meeting held at Los Llanos air base in Albacete, the headquarters of the Republican *Jefatura de la Zona Aérea Centro-Sur*.

Negrín, supported by the Communists, started a series of changes in commanders who opposed his desires of extreme resistance. In Madrid, after contacting the leaders of political parties and trade unions, *coronel* Segismundo Casado, chief of the *Ejército del Centro*, upon hearing of his dismissal as commander of this large organization and his subsequent posting to the General Staff, decided to rebel and establish a *Consejo Nacional de Defensa*. All of those he contacted, except for the Communist Party, supported him. *General* José Miaja assumed presidency of the council.

1939: THE END OF THE SPANISH CIVIL WAR

A Farman monoplane, coded '30-30', in the foreground with a Czech Aero A 101 light bomber behind, seen at Leon.

Reconnaissance and close-support Heinkel He 45s were used both by the Legion Condor and the Nationalist aviation. Seen here in flight is '15-25' of Grupo 6G-15. ('Canario' Azaola)

Heinkel He 45, coded 15-21, Kette (H) A./88, Legion Condor
Although most Heinkel He 45s were handed over to the Spanish, who used them to equip Grupo 6G-15, the Germans also used these aircraft in the Kette (H) of the A./88, on tactical reconnaissance and artillery-ranging sorties, as was the case with '15-21'.

Between 6 and 11 March 1939, there was a fierce struggle in Madrid between supporters of *coronel* Casado and the Communists. The Republican aviation, headed by its chief commander, *coronel* Antonio Camacho, supported Casado, who was also supported by aviation *coronel* Manuel Cascón Briega, who had been unattached in Madrid for a long time.

On the 9th and 10th, the government Polikarpov RZ *Natacha* and Tupolev SB *Katiuska* aircraft, operating on the side of Casado, flew several bombing sorties on communication centres, such as the Madrid-Alcalá de Henares road, the Fuencarral-Canillejas junction, and the Communist barracks at El Pardo. They also dropped leaflets over the Chamartín neighbourhood, asking the Communists to lay down arms.

AIR WAR OVER SPAIN

An excellent in-flight view of two escuadrillas of Savoia SM.81s. (J. Salas)

A Polikarpov I-15 ready to take off from an advanced airstrip.

Eventually, *coronel* Casado managed to control the situation and quickly made approaches to start negotiations with the Nationalists. On 19 March, *general* Franco accepted these secret negotiations which were held in Burgos, where the Republican envoys flew in a Douglas DC-2. Surrender of aircraft was arranged for the 25th, which could not be done. The negotiations were thus cancelled, with no practical results.

Almost simultaneously with *coronel* Casado's coup against Negrín, other attempted coups followed at the Naval base at Cartagena by the *Infantería de Marina*, *Artillería de Costa* and *Marina* forces, which were suppressed with aid from an aviation ground column from Los Alcázares and San Javier and an infantry brigade.

The flight and surrender of the Republican aviation

On 5 March 1939, after the departure from Cartagena of the government fleet, the command of the *Escuadrilla Mixta de Cooperación* decided to follow it and took off from El Carmolí in Murcia and landed in the Oran-La Sénia air base in French Algeria at 1700 hrs. This formation comprised one Potez 540, two Vultee V-1 As and a González Gil GP.1 Especial light plane, with 36 airmen.

On the following day, given the political situation, President Negrín decided to abandon Spain and head for France, with a part of the government, which boarded two Douglas DC-2s. Other politicians of lesser rank and senior military officers who had no seats in these aircraft would not be able to reach France, so they decided to head for the air base at Oran in French Algeria using two De Havilland DH-89 Dragon Rapides, which carried *general* Antonio Cordón, *coronel subsecretario de Aviación* Carlos Núñez Maza, Soviet advisor Rodion Malinovski, four officers and the writers Rafael Alberti and María Teresa León, along with Communist leaders Jesús Monzón and Dolores Ibárruri, '*La Pasionaria.*'

1939: THE END OF THE SPANISH CIVIL WAR

German Arado Ar 68s were used as night fighters at the end of the conflict from La Cenia air base. (Campesino, via Raúl Arias)

Comandantes Joaquín García Morato and Ángel Salas Larrazábal, two of the Nationalists' best fighter pilots.

Comandante García Morato, the leading ace of the Spanish Civil War with 40 kills, climbs out of his aircraft, Fiat CR.32 '3-51'. (Calparsoro)

83

AIR WAR OVER SPAIN

Obsolete Potez 25s were relegated to coastal defence with the Republican Grupo nº 71.

Fiat CR.32 '3-61' was the usual aircraft of the Nationalist ace, Ángel Salas Larrazábal. (Salgado)

1939: THE END OF THE SPANISH CIVIL WAR

On 7 March, a further two aircraft, including a Vultee V.1 A, landed in Oran with the correspondents of the *News Chronicle* and *L'Ordre* newspapers.

A second wave of Republican aircraft fled to French Algeria on 24 and 25 March 1939. On the 24th, two aircraft of the *Escuela de Polimotores* at Totana, Murcia, namely a De Havilland DH-90 Dragonfly and a De Havilland DH-89 Dragon Rapide, landed in Tigdit, near Mostaganen. Other aircraft of the same types landed five kilometres from Sidi-Bel-Abbes. On board these aircraft were several politicians and leaders of the Communist Party, including Jesús Hernández, Vicente Uribe, Pedro Checa, José Palau, Isidoro Diéguez, Palmiro Togliatti and Virgilio Llanos. Also with them were some military men, including *mayor* Artemio Precioso, commander of the *206ª Brigada Mixta*, two captains and the commissar of the *206ª Brigada*, Victoriano Sánchez.

On the 25th, six training aircraft of the *Escuela de Caza* at Lorca, Murcia including three De Havilland DH-82 Tiger Moths, landed in a vineyard, and three Caudron C.600 Aiglons landed at the Oran-La Sénia air base. Several student pilots without too serious political tendencies were flying in them.

The skeletal remains of a Polikarpov I-15 which was the victim of a strafing attack at Vilajuiga air base in Gerona in February 1939.

Leocadio Mendiola Núñez
(Badajoz, 1909 – Extremadura, 1998)

In 1930, Leocadio Mendiola Núñez was posted to the Cuatro Vientos air base in Madrid and joined *general* Queipo de Llano's unsuccessful Republican uprising. Mendiola was jailed until the advent of the 2nd Republic. He qualified as a pilot in 1932. In 1936 he was posted to the *1ª Escuadrilla* of the *Grupo nº 31 de reconocimiento estratégico* at Getafe. On 18 July, *brigada* Mendiola reconnoitred and bombed the Getafe and Carabanchel rebel barracks flying Breguet XIXs and then operated over the Sierra and Extremadura fronts. He distinguished himself bombing rebel columns on the Peguerinos front, forcing the enemy to retreat to Avila. Promoted *teniente* in October 1936, during the defence of Madrid, and very shortly afterwards mentioned in dispatches, Mendiola was promoted *capitán* in December.

In November 1936, after multi-engine training, Mendiola joined the Tupolev SB *Katiuska*-equipped *2ª Escuadrilla* of *Grupo nº 12*, one of the first Spaniards to do so. He flew bombing sorties over the enemy rearguard during the winter and in the battle of the Jarama was often mentioned in dispatches. In May 1937, Mendiola assumed command of the *3ª Escuadrilla* of *Grupo nº 24 de Katiuskas* and took part in many battles including La Granja, Brunete and Belchite. His most relevant sorties were the bombings of the enemy air bases at Burgos, Saragossa and Villarcayo. Promoted *mayor* and mentioned in dispatches in November 1937, he assumed command of *Grupo nº 24*.

On 6 March 1938, Mendiola led the bombing of the ships rescuing the survivors of the sunken cruiser *Baleares*. He was recommended for the *Placa Laureada de Madrid*, but the closing of the *Diario Oficial* did not allow him to see publication of the official approval. On 15 December, Mendiola was promoted *teniente coronel* and mentioned in dispatches. He then led the attack by two *Katiuska* squadrons on the *Legion Condor* air base at La Cenia, losing two aircraft, including one of the *escuadrilla* commanders. After the fall of Catalonia, Mendiola fled to France. Back in Spain, he resumed command of *Grupo nº 24*. After *coronel* Casado's coup, Mendiola was appointed military commander of Murcia, but he could not report, for fear of being arrested or murdered, as the government had actually fled the country. Ordered to surrender the government aircraft to the Nationalist victors, Mendiola decided to exile and flew a *Katiuska* to Oran. He was interned and volunteered for the RAF with other fellow airmen to fight the Germans, but they were not accepted. Mendiola remained in Algeria until 1942, then managed to leave for Mexico, where he lived until 1967, after which he returned to his native country.

Teniente coronel Mendiola, the only airman to be awarded the Placa Laureada de Madrid, in the cockpit of his Katiuska.

The staff of Grupo nº 24. From left to right: Antonio Tellería (chief armourer), Jaime Vallhonrat (chief of ground crew), Francisco Vega (commissar), Leocadio Mendiola (Grupo commanding officer), Adrián Bragado (chief of staff), Juan Caldevilla (chief observer), Domingo Bonilla (chief air gunner).

AIR WAR OVER SPAIN

Polikarpov RZ Natachas were the real workhorses of the Republican aviation's light bombing force. (Coello)

The pilot of a Polikarpov RZ Natacha biplane light bomber poses for a photograph in the aircraft's cockpit.

De Havilland DH-89 Dragon Rapides of the Republican Escuela de Polimotores at Totana, Murcia, 1938.

1939: THE END OF THE SPANISH CIVIL WAR

Potez 542 coded 'R' was one of the longest-serving aircraft with Escuadrilla de Polimotores of Grupo nº 72.

Potez 540, 'A', Madrid Front, November 1936
These French twin-engined aircraft served initially with the Grupo Potez, which included Malraux's Escuadrilla 'España', in 1936 and early 1937. Shortly afterwards, they were handed over to Grupo nº 11 and then to Grupo Mixto nº 72, where they became part of the Escuadrilla de Polimotores. This bomber, coded 'A' and flown by the Italo-Soviet Primo Gibelli, was shot down by the Nationalist anti-aircraft artillery on the Madrid front, on 10 November 1936.

The third and last great escape by government aircraft took place on 28 and 29 March 1939. On the 28th, 11 Polikarpov RZ *Natachas* of the *1ª Escuadrilla* of *Grupo nº 30*, with 48 airmen, politicians and military leaders on board, landed at the Oran-La Sénia air base, arriving from San Pedro de Pinatar, Murcia. At 0830 hrs on the 29th, a Latécoère 281 from Los Alcázares, Murcia with 12 airmen on board, landed at the Algerian air base.

At 1100 hrs a further two aircraft landed from Manises, Valencia, one of them carrying *teniente coronel* Cipriano Mera as passenger. In the afternoon, another aircraft landed, carrying the Communist youth leaders Segismundo Álvarez, Ignacio Gallego, Fernando Claudín, Sebastián Zapiraín and Josefina López.

On the following day, no fewer than 24 Republican aircraft arrived in Oran, with 70 airmen and officers. At around 0845 hrs, four Polikarpov I-15 *Chatos*, five Grumman GE-23 *Delfíns* and seven Polikarpov R-5 *Rasantes* landed at La Senia. They belonged to *4ª* and *5ª Escuadrillas* of *Grupo Mixto nº 71*, led by *capitán* José Riverola. A Polikarpov RZ *Natacha,* flown by *mayor* José María del Romero Fernández, commander of *Grupo nº 30* came in as did a transport aircraft with *teniente coronel* Luis Alonso Vega, Chief-of-Staff of the *Zona Aérea del Centro-Sur*, and *mayor* Antonio Molina Sánchez, commander of the *1ª Región Aérea*.

At 1100 hrs, a further two aircraft landed; one of them was an unidentified transport aircraft and the other was an Airspeed AS.6 III Envoy, with *capitán piloto* José Corrochano Márquez, *general* José

87

Miaja Menat, *teniente coronel* José Pérez Martínez and *mayor* Mario Páramo Roldán; the latter were the general's aides.

At 1230 hrs, the last four government aircraft landed at La Senia, from Los Llanos led by *teniente coronel* Leocadio Mendiola Núñez, commander of *Grupo n° 24*. They included two Tupolev SB *Katiuskas*; one flown by Mendiola and the other by *capitán* Ananías Sanjuán. A third SB *Katiuska* landed at Tigditt, near Mostaganen, flown by *teniente* Santiago Ramón Prior García, commander of the *Escuadrilla de Entrenamiento* (Training Squadron) of that group.

Once the civil war was over, 59 government aircraft were recovered in French Algeria, as follows:

Combat aircraft	
Polikarpov RZ *Natacha*	13
Polikarpov R.5 *Rasante*	7
Polikarpov I-15 *Chato*	5
Grumman GE. 23 *Delfin*	5
Tupolev SB *Katiuska*	3
Vultee V.1 A	3
Potez 540	1
Subtotal	37
Transport and training aircraft	
De Havilland DH-89 Dragon Rapide	6
Consolidated 20 A Fleetster	2
Nothrop Delta	1
Lockheed L.9 Orion	1
Latécoère Laté 281	1
Airspeed AS-6 Envoy	1
Subtotal	12
Training aircraft	
De Havilland DH-82 Tiger Moth	4
Caudron C.600 Aiglon	3
González Gil GP.1	3
Subtotal	10
Total	**59**

On 29 March, finally and with no political concessions, the rest of the units of the Republican aviation surrendered symbolically at Barajas air base in Madrid. One of the airmen who surrendered there, *teniente observador* Fernando Medina, recalled: 'On 29 March we were ordered to surrender at Barajas, for, according to our aviation chiefs, this was inevitable if we wanted to see our status as combatants acknowledged. We, by the way, had had the same chances as our other comrades but did not make good use of them and returned to face an uncertain fate.

'We took off from San Clemente – nine *Katiuskas* and six [I-15s] of Tarazona's[1] – and landed in the early hours at Barajas. So did twelve *Chatos* and some twenty *Natachas*. We lined up in front of the aircraft and an officer reviewed us. We had not fallen out yet as three Messerschmitts landed, one being flown by Richthofen, who inspected the aircraft with Kindelán and *don* Alfonso de Orleáns. They exchanged some words, not exactly kind, with Joaquín Calvo, chief of the Republican fighter force. We were ordered to line up and take off our flying suits, including our leather flight jackets. We protested, but to no avail and all of it was handed out to their soldiers.'

In fact, the aircraft that arrived at Barajas were fourteen Tupolev SB *Katiuskas*, sixteen Polikarpov RZ *Natachas* and nine Polikarpov I-15 *Chatos*.

Peace at last
Once Catalonia was taken by the *Ejército del Norte*, Azaña resigned as President of the Republic and Vicente Rojo did the same as Chief-of-Staff. The war was lost for the Republicans and so understood *coronel* Casado, who forced Prime Minister Negrín to flee.

Before the Italians and Germans went home, there was a huge air parade at Barajas with some 450 aircraft and shortly afterwards the new *Ejército del Aire* was born.

[1.] Tarazona was the commander of *3ª Escuadrilla de Moscas*.

1939: THE END OF THE SPANISH CIVIL WAR

Aircrew and ground crew of the Republican Escuadrilla Vultee of Grupo nº 72 pose for a photograph in front of one of their Vultee V1As.

A group of pilots of the government's Escuela de Caza posing with a Chato and Mosca.

AIR WAR OVER SPAIN

The Chato seen here, flown by sargento Arranz, landed deliberately at the enemy air base at La Cenia. The Germans subsequently painted over the government markings.

A Caudron C.600 Aiglon light aircraft of the government's Escuela de Vuelo. Standing up in the forward compartment wearing white overalls is the Yugoslav volunteer, Josip Krizaj or Giuseppe Crisay, as he was known variously.

Surrendered Tupolev SBs at Barajas at the end of the war.

1939: THE END OF THE SPANISH CIVIL WAR

A government Polikarpov R.Z Natacha which appears to have either surrendered or been abandoned.

Two photographs of government aircraft abandoned at the French air base at Francazal, Toulouse in 1940: a Fokker F-VII nº 16 EC-UAA in the foreground and a Dragon Rapide (above) and a LAPE Caudron Goëland (right).

This Caudron Goëland, coded '31-2', was captured at Zarauz and used as a liaison aircraft by the Nationalists.

At the end of the civil war in Spain, there was a mass parade at Barajas air base involving some 450 aircraft, presided over by general Franco. (J. Salas)

APPENDICES

Appendix I

Military ranks (pilots and aircrew) in the *Aviación Militar* and RAF approximate equivalents

General de aviación	Air Commodore
Coronel	Group Captain
Teniente coronel	Wing Commander
Comandante (during the war, the title was replaced with that of *mayor* on the Republican side)	Squadron Leader
Capitán	Flight Lieutenant
Teniente piloto	Flying Officer (Pilot)
Teniente observador	Flying Officer (Observer)
Teniente	Flying Officer
Alférez piloto	Pilot Officer (Pilot)
Alférez observador	Pilot Officer (Observer)
Alférez bombardero	Pilot Officer (Bombardier)
Alférez	Pilot Officer (Reserve)
Alférez de complemento	Pilot Officer
Subteniente	Warrant Officer
Suboficial piloto	Warrant Officer (Reserve Pilot)
Suboficial de reserva	Warrant Officer (Reserve)
Suboficial de complemento	Warrant Officer (Reserve)
Brigada piloto	Warrant Officer (Pilot)
Brigada radio aéreo	Warrant Officer (Wireless Operator)
Brigada mecánico	Warrant Officer (Engineer)
Sargento piloto	Sergeant (Pilot)
Sargento mecánico	Sergeant (Engineer)
Sargento de complemento	Sergeant (Reserve)
Cabo piloto	Corporal (Pilot)
Cabo mecánico	Corporal (Engineer)
Cabo	Corporal
Soldado piloto	Airman (Pilot)
Soldado mecánico	Airman (Engineer)
Soldado	Airman

Military ranks of pilots and aircrew in the *Aeronáutica Naval* and RN approximate equivalents

Capitán de corbeta piloto	*Lieutenant-Commander (Pilot)*
Capitán de corbeta observador naval	*Lieutenant-Commander (Observer)*
Capitán de corbeta	*Lieutenant-Commander*
Teniente de navío piloto	*Lieutenant (Pilot)*
Teniente de navío observador naval	*Lieutenant (Observer)*
Teniente de navío	*Lieutenant*
Alférez de navío piloto	*Sub-Lieutenant (Pilot)*
Alférez de navío observador naval	*Sub-Lieutenant (Observer)*
Alférez de navío	*Sub-Lieutenant*
Cuerpo Auxiliar de Aeronáutica	*Air Arm Auxiliary Corps*
Oficial 1° piloto	*Similar to Lieutenant (Pilot)*
Oficial 1° observador	*Similar to Lieutenant (Observer)*
Oficial 1° mecánico	*Similar to Lieutenant (Engineer)*
Oficial 2° piloto	*Similar to Sub-Lieutenant (Pilot)*
Oficial 2° observador	*Similar to Sub-Lieutenant (Observer)*
Oficial 2° mecánico	*Similar to Sub-Lieutenant (Engineer)*
Oficial 3° piloto	*Similar to Midshipman (Pilot)*
Oficial 3° observador	*Similar to Midshipman (Observer)*
Auxiliar 1° piloto	*Similar to Fleet Chief Petty Officer (Pilot)*
Auxiliar 1° observador	*Similar to Fleet Chief Petty Officer (Observer)*

Auxiliar 1° mecánico	Similar to Fleet Chief Petty Officer (Engineer)
Auxiliar 2° piloto	--
Auxiliar 2° observador	--
Auxiliar 2° mecánico	--
Contramaestre piloto	Chief Petty Officer (Pilot)
Contramaestre observador	Chief Petty Officer (Observer)
Contramaestre mecánico	Chief Petty Officer (Engineer)
2° Contramaestre piloto	Petty Officer (Pilot)
2° Contramaestre observador	Petty Officer (Observer)
2° Contramaestre mecánico	Petty Officer (Engineer)
Maestre piloto	Leading Seaman (Pilot)
Maestre observador	Leading Seaman (Observer)
Maestre mecánico	Leading Seaman (Engineer)
Cabo piloto	Able Seaman (Pilot)
Cabo observador	Able Seaman (Observer)
Cabo mecánico	Able Seaman (Engineer)

A portrait of an officer wearing the typical uniform of a mayor in the Republican Aviación Militar.

Appendix II

UNIFORMS

With the advent of the 2nd Republic, the *Aviación Militar*, now established as an Arm, received a new navy blue uniform, very similar to that of the *Marina*, which featured once again the classic stars and cuff stripes.

With the outbreak of the Civil War, the Republican aviation reintroduced chevrons – briefly used in the 1920s – in order to distinguish the ranks of senior and junior officers and NCOs, and retained the navy blue uniform of the Republic, utilising a white version during summer months.

The Nationalist aviation retained the traditional four-, eight- and six-point stars. In 1938 the rebel aviation created a new uniform, light blue in colour.

It was not until the creation of the *Ejército del Aire* in 1939 that the blue uniform became standard and, with small variations, it has remained in use to the present day.

A member of the Republican Aviación Militar in the uniform of the Servicios de Instrucción y Material at Cuatro Vientos. The letters on the man's cap should not be confused with those of the Servicio de Información Militar.

A group of Soviet pilots in Spain. In the centre, wearing the uniform of a capitán of the Spanish aviation is Ivan Yeromenko.

Groundcrew of the 3ª Escuadrilla of Grupo n° 24 assemble in their dress uniform for a commemorative photograph.

DECORATIONS

The *Cruz Laureada de San Fernando* is the highest decoration in the Spanish armed forces, followed by the *Medalla Militar Individual*, which has a collective version called the *Medalla Militar Colectiva*, awarded to distinguished units: it is not actually a medal, but an arm badge that is worn on the sleeve. The third decoration is the *Cruz del Mérito Militar con distintivo rojo* and finally the *Medalla de Campaña*. These decorations were awarded to Nationalist airmen during the war, including Germans and Italians.

In the loyalist area, regulations were changed and the *Cruz Laureada de San Fernando* became the *Placa Laureada de Madrid*. Other decorations created during the war were the *Medalla al Valor* and the *Medalla del Deber*. However, procedures were too slow to start with and hardly any were actually awarded. Mentions in dispatches followed by promotions in rank were the most common effective award.

German and Italian airmen in Spain maintained their own decorations. The former established a specific decoration known as the *Spanien Kreuz*, with different categories.

Italian 'Gamba di Ferro' emblem

APPENDICES

Soviet airmen also maintained their own decorations, which were awarded upon their return to the USSR.

EMBLEMS AND BADGES

During the Civil War, colourful and artistic emblems proliferated on Nationalist aircraft, including those on the Italian or German air units. To describe such emblems in detail would require much space, the Italian '*Asso di Bastoni*', '*La Cucaracha*' or '*Gamba di Ferro*', or the German '*Zylinderhut*', or the most popular '*Mickey Mouse*' should be mentioned. Personal or individual emblems also proliferated, particularly those used by the German or Italian pilots, rather than the Spanish.

With some exceptions, the government aviation, certainly influenced by austere Soviet habits, did not display many unit emblems; however the penguin of the 2ª *Escuadrilla de 'Chatos'* or the 4ª *Escuadrilla de 'Moscas'* Popeye are examples of those that were used. The 'Mickey Mouse' was also used by *capitán* Vicente Castillo Monzó, CO of the 1ª *Escuadrilla* of the *Grupo de Chatos*.

Some of these emblems that originated during the Civil War, such as that of *comandante* García Morato's bullfighting '*Suerte, Vista and al Toro*' cry of *Grupo de Caza 2G-3*, have survived to this day.

MARKINGS

At the time of the 2nd Republic, the Spanish red-yellow-red flag underwent a transformation, as the lower band became purple. For that reason, both the national flag painted on the rudder of Spanish military aircraft and the inner circle of the badge on the upper and lower wing surfaces, underwent a similar change.

During the civil conflict, in order to differentiate the aircraft of the same type or model, but fighting on different sides, Republican aircraft used a wide red band on the wings and fuselage and the tricolour flag on the rudder.

The Nationalists painted over the Republican badges and flag with black paint and that was the birth of the current St Andrew's cross on the rudder of military aircraft. Later, black circles and bands were added on the wings and fuselage. With peace, the new *Ejército del Aire* maintained the St Andrew's cross on the rudder and recovered the bicolour badge, which have remained to this day.

MILITARISED CIVIL AVIATION

As noted in the narrative text, the L.A.P.E. Fokker F-VII 3ms, the Ford F.5 and the Douglas DC-2 were used by both government/Republican and rebel/Nationalists as makeshift bombers during the early months of the Civil War, and they were even fitted with defensive armament, consisting of movable machine guns. On the government side, the most remarkable missions were the bombing raids against enemy airfields in North Africa, Leon and Logroño, as well as the attacks on the Naval Base at El Ferrol, where the modern *Canarias* and *Baleares* cruisers were being built. With the arrival of the new Tupolev SB *Katiuska* bombers, the DC-2s returned to their usual transport missions and liaison flights to the north or to neighbouring France.

With the outbreak of the Civil War, the military authorities on both sides seized virtually all light and sport aircraft, both those in aero clubs and in private hands.

Private pilots were quickly mobilized or transformed into military pilots at the flying schools that were soon established, because of the huge growing numbers of military aircraft being used in the conflict.

On the Nationalist side, it was the *Aero Club de Sevilla* which established the first *Escuela de Vuelo Militar* in the area, because all of the *Servicios de Instrucción* – Training Services – were in government territory.

As regards the Republican side, the autonomous authorities of Catalonia established a short-lived *Escuela de Pilotos Militares* in Barcelona, as the central government wisely decided to assume the whole of aviation services.

AIRCREW TRAINING

Both fighting sides had to set about the task of training military pilots in large numbers, as the conflict intensified and resulted in heavy aircrew casualties and losses.

In the government area there were the *Servicios de Instrucción*, embracing the schools for pilots, observers, air gunners and bombers, mechanics, radio operators, and photographers. The schools in the Madrid area were soon moved to the Levante area in the Mediterranean.

In spite of the good work of these schools, the Spanish government was granted permission from the French government to authorise basic training to be carried out there, but this did not extend to military training, which was completed in Spain.

It was the Soviet Union which assured the Republicans full training for the Spanish airmen. Thus, from early 1937 to the end of the Civil War, five groups of Spanish pilots and observers were trained in Russia, of which only four got back to Spain in time to take part in the conflict.

The 'Zylinderhut' (top hat) emblem of Jagdgruppe 88, which was carried by both He 51s and Bf 109s of the Legion Condor.

A Mickey Mouse emblem appeared in different incarnations on several German aircraft in Spain. This example adorned the He 51 of Heinrich Neumann, a medical officer flying with 3.J/88 of the Legion Condor.

The Mickey Mouse which was carried on the Bf 109 D-1 flown by Hptm. Werner Mölders, Staffelkapitän of 3.J/88 in November 1938.

Nationalist fighter pilots wearing dress uniform on the day that comandante García Morato was awarded the Cruz Laureada de San Fernando.

Italian 'Asso di Bastoni' emblem

Capitán Vicente Castillo of 1ª Escuadrilla, Grupo n° 26 posing by the tail of Chato 'CA-141' adorned with his personal Mickey Mouse emblem.

Italian 'La Cucaracha' emblem

AIR WAR OVER SPAIN

In Nationalist Spain, military *Escuelas de Vuelo* were established at Seville, Badajoz and Jerez de la Frontera airfields, but some Spanish pilots were also sent to Germany and Italy, where they received excellent aeronautical training.

AIR MERCENARIES: HEROES OR VILLAINS?

The Spanish Civil War brought in waves of idealists to both sides. The confrontation between foreign mercenary airmen who chose between democracy and fascism also materialized in Spanish aviation, although this applied to the government side more.

The position of these air adventurers was epitomized by French writer, André Malraux, who was later minister with *général* Charles De Gaulle.

Malraux, who was not actually an airman, was the visible leader of what was known as the '*Escuadrilla España*', which was home for a brief time for airmen from many different European countries – from France to the Soviet Union, although there were even *white* Russians for a time in this short-lived unit.

Although many have idealized the persona of Malraux, seeing him as a sort of contemporary Lord Byron, the government air command was not very satisfied with the adventures of these purported airmen.

There was a small group of American pilots who fought on the Republican side and although some of them, such as Frank Tinker or Albert Baumler, became aces, there were others like Harold Dahl, who was taken prisoner by the Francoists, and did not hesitate in offering his services to *general* Franco, as he regarded himself as a mercenary fighting for money.

ENEMIES IN BATTLE; GENTLEMEN TO THE END

A civil war would not seem to be the best place to preserve old acquaintances among military men fighting on different sides. However, during the Spanish Civil War there were a number of examples which deserve mention when chivalry was not at odds with the respective ideals.

Such was the friendship between *generales* Alfredo Kindelán y Duany and Emilio Herrera Linares, two senior *Aviación* officers serving on different sides, both from the Engineers Corps of the 1st Military Pilots' Year. The former, chief of the Nationalist aviation, kindly forwarded the possessions of *sargento piloto* Emilio Herrera Aguilera – the latter's son, who was killed in action flying an I-15 *Chato* over enemy territory – to his afflicted father in the Republican zone. In spite of fighting on opposing sides, both airmen respected, admired and loved each other.

Another case of chivalry in the air should also be mentioned. Nationalist *comandante* Ángel Salas Larrazábal shot down four enemy aircraft in combat over the Extremadura front on 2 September 1938. He saluted and protected Republican *teniente piloto* José Redondo Martín, commander of the *1ª Escuadrilla de Moscas*, when the latter was going down unharmed in his parachute until he landed.

MOST DISTINGUISHED AIR UNITS

Certainly, all of the operational air units distinguished themselves more than once throughout the civil conflict in Spain but, on the other hand, as an author's viewpoint can always be subjective, we shall list here the *escuadras*, *grupos* or *escuadrillas* which received an official award.

As regards Nationalist aviation, the CR.32-equipped *2G-3* and *3G-3* Spanish fighter groups, as well as the '*cadena*' He 51-equipped *1G-2* and He 45-equipped *6G-15* groups received a collective *Medalla Militar*. Similarly, the Ju 52-equipped *Escuadra nº 1 de bombardeo*, made up of Spanish airmen, received the same collective decoration.

The Italian fighter groups, '*La Cucaracha*' or '*Asso di Bastoni*' were awarded the same collective decoration.

It should be noticed that, despite their remarkable successes, the German groups or squadrons of the *Legion Condor* did not receive group decorations.

As regards the Republican *Aviación Militar*, it hardly ever awarded decorations. As an exception however, the I-15-equipped *1ª Escuadrilla* of *Grupo nº 26* was awarded the *Medalla al Valor*, in recognition of its distinguished service while conducting strafing missions on the Catalonia front during the final phase of the Spanish Civil War.